THE FOXFIRE BOOK
OF WINEMAKING

THE FOXFIRE BOOK OF WINEMAKING

Recipes and Memories
in the Appalachian Tradition

STUDENT EDITORS
Lori Gillespie, Kelly Shropshire, and Allison Adams

STAFF COORDINATORS
Hilton Smith and Margie Bennett

STUDENT STAFF
*Donna Ramey, Annmarie Lee, Marty Veal, Kim White,
Felrese Bradshaw, Bud Carroll, Joseph Fowler, Kevin Fountain,
Hedy Davalos, Mark Edwards, Teresa Thurmond, Tricia Leavens,
Clark Bowen, Oh Soon Shropshire, Karen Key, Chet Welch,
Dawn Watson, Robin Lakey, Richard Edwards*

COVER PHOTO
Al Edwards

REPRODUCTION EDITOR
Ann Moore

REPRODUCTION DESIGN
Lee Carpenter

Originally Published in 1987

Copyright © 1987, 2008 by The Foxfire Fund, Inc.

Published in the United States by The Foxfire Fund, Inc.
P. O. Box 541, Mountain City, Georgia 30562-0541

ISBN-13: 978-0-9821397-0-7 (paperback)
ISBN-10: 0-9821397-0-5 (paperback)

CONTENTS

INTRODUCTION

For many people of the Appalachian mountains, winemaking is as much a part of their culture as the mountains themselves. Made from the fruits and berries native to the land, homemade wine has been used for everything from curing stomachaches to cooking and, of course, just plain drinking.

While winemaking is generally thought of as being centralized in the Napa Valley region of California, and the hills of upstate New York, its roots actually have been traced back to our European ancestors, who brought the craft over from the Old World. Many of these early settlers came to the South and brought with them the ancient methods of winemaking. Despite admonitions against the evils of strong drink by Bible Belt preachers, winemaking caught on. Over the years, many unique winemaking methods, as well as types, have evolved. There are those like Lawton Brooks, who use the natural yeast on the fruit itself to make their muscadine wine. And others, like Granny Toothman, who refuse to make their wine in anything but a stone jar. Blackberry, dandelion, corncob—the types of Appalachian wines are as diverse as the people who make them.

We first became interested in winemaking during preparation of *The Foxfire Book of Appalachian Cookery*. We began learning of mountain people who still made their own wines at home from the fruit they had grown themselves. Over and over again, the subject came up. Finally, it dawned on us that after twenty years of researching and recording the Appalachian heritage, here was something we'd never done before—a documentation of winemaking in the southern Appalachian mountains. Toting tape recorders and cameras, we set out on our interviews and were amazed at what we discovered—and we usually found ourselves directly involved in the winemaking process. We gathered grapes for Bill Park, crushed blackberries for Harry Pitts, and gutted a pumpkin for Effie Lord. We found that the various types of wine were endless—as John Bulgin puts it, "You can make wine out of anything but a rock."

Now, we offer to you our finished product. This is a book for the amateur winemaker interested in learning the skill, as well as for the experienced winemaker interested in unearthing the roots of winemaking in this region. And most important, in the tradition of Foxfire, this is a book intended to preserve a small piece of our heritage and to pass along the traditions of the people of the southern Appalachian mountains.

This book is divided up into three sections. The first is a narrative section—the transcripts of our interviews with the Appalachian winemaking folk. This section introduces you to these people: You hear their own winemaking stories, told while actually making the wine. We have arranged this narrative section to begin with the simple, basic methods of making wine (natural yeasts and basic equipment), moving to more complex methods (the use of hydrometers, air locks, and chemicals).

Due to the nature of the dialogue—casual and sometimes meandering speech—we urge you to use the second and third sections to actually make your wine.

The second section, "For Best Results," is an information and technical section to help prospective winemakers make the transition from the narrative to the actual recipe section. It includes informative yet simple notes on equipment, ingredients, air locks, chemicals, the use of the hydrometer, etc., and should be read before attempting to make *any* wine.

The third section, "Recipes," consists of the actual recipes given to us by the people of the mountains (the recipes described in the narrative section). This section, like the technical section, has been designed to be as simple as possible, with very direct instructions and basic language. Included in the recipe section are several juice recipes, as well as recipes for other beverages, including homebrew, mead, and persimmon beer.

Now it's up to you. As you can see by looking at the recipe section, there is a great variety of wines to choose from—and the choice is entirely yours. As R. C. Dobbins says, "The hardest thing about making wine is that it takes time." But when you taste the result and feel the pleasure of having made a good wine—and the pride of helping keep a tradition alive—we believe the time and energy spent will be worth it.

—Kelly Shropshire

INTERVIEWS

"Wine is the easiest stuff made."

~LAWTON BROOKS~

I was raised in Clay County, North Carolina, and when I married I went to Macon County, North Carolina. I stayed there until I came to Georgia, and I've been in Georgia ever since—pretty close to fifty years. Once I got here I just couldn't leave!

[The first place I lived in Georgia was] Dillard. I ran a gristmill there for about three years for Mrs. Brown. Then I farmed and worked around—I forget how long I did. Then I worked for the [Rabun Gap-Nacoochee] School. I farmed here and stayed ten years with them. My job was to keep the campus up. I used to do all this mowing here with mules—we didn't have but one tractor. I mowed this hill right here. I even set these trees up. I don't see how they growed that big in that length of time. Don't seem like too long ago, but it's been a durn long time. Time runs fast when you get old. Time done left you then. Don't have birthdays much when you're as young as you are. When you get old, they come in bunches!

I commenced makin' wine when I was about twenty-two years old. Started with elderberry wine. Me and a feller got started drinking wine and he said, "Why don't we try to make some?" And when I commenced on it, I didn't get my first wine too good, so I just doctored it up a little. I threw some more sugar to it and worked it a little longer and got it to where it'd knock you down. It'd kill a man!

Wine is the easiest stuff made, Honey, of anything I know. You can make wine out of almost anything that will sour. I've made elderberry wine, blackberry wine, muscadine wine, all kinds of grape wine. The best wine I ever made was made out of muscadines. If you was to taste it, you'd drink it, too. The best-tastin' stuff you ever tasted in your life! Anybody'd drink it!

If you are making a muscadine or blackberry wine, you'll want to put your grapes or berries in a churn and mash them up good. Let them set three days and they'll work. Just put them up today and go back tomorrow and see if they're working. If they ain't, just let 'em alone and go back the next day. You can tell when they go to working. You don't add no sugar for your first working of your stuff. After that three days, you strain the juice all out through a cloth where there won't be no seeds or nothing in it. Then you measure the juice and put 2½ to 3 pounds of sugar to the gallon of juice. You can add yeast, but I never did to mine. I didn't want any in it.

Then, let it set back awhile. In about three days, it'll be worked again. You don't want to let it work too awful long. (If you do, it'll turn just like vinegar and you can't drink it.) If you want to make it really strong, to drink it and get drunk, you can go back again and add a little more sugar to it. That makes it have more alcohol in it. You can make it stout!

When it's working, you'll want to cover it. Tie a cheesecloth around the top to keep those ol' gnats out, but it will give the wine some air.

Some people make wine in barrels. Any kind of ol' crock or wooden barrel would be fine. They take a big ol' wooden barrel and fill it full of grapes or whatever they're making wine from. If you have a great big ol' wooden barrel, you might run out 10 or 12 gallons of juice. Or if a man had a little 5-gallon keg with the head knocked out of it, that'd be fine, too. Used to, they mostly made wine in wooden kegs. Some of them had a spigot and you could turn it and run your wine right in the glass.

I don't know if I'd want to make any in a dadblamed metal container or not. When that wine works, it makes a lot of acid and it could get something off that metal in it. I'd be afraid to try it with a metal pot!

It's better to make wine in the summertime. Warm as it is nowadays, like it's been a'being—good God, you put it up today and tomorrow, that stuff will start working. You don't want to set it out in the hot sun. You just want to set it in the shade where it will be cool. But in the wintertime, you've got to keep it in your house. It won't hardly start working if you set it outside somewhere where it stays cold. It's got to be a certain temperature to get it to

Lawton Brooks

working.

I've drunk bought wine, but I don't like it. I just don't like the taste of it. Why, a fellow tried to give me a quart here just a few days ago. I told him I couldn't drink that. If it had been homemade wine, I'd've took it.

Wine won't hurt you unless you just make a hog out of yourself, if you don't ever get drunk. I like to drink me a glass every once in a while. It ain't gonna bother you a bit in the world if you just take you a common glass of wine and go on about your business. It's a good medicine, but if you don't use it right, it ain't no good to you.

Well, you could use wine for many different things. You could use wine in your cooking. A lot of people use wine in their cakes, you know. We had people who would go crazy about a wine-soaked cake—soak their cakes in wine. I never did like cake mixed with wine. I don't know why. It just didn't taste right with that cake.

Old folks kept wine. They had all kinds. If they had some kind of a gathering, something like a birthday or parties, they'd get their wine out and they'd all take a little glass. Nobody didn't drink enough to feel it, you know. Back then, that was fine. Those old people wouldn't let the children have a drink of wine. They never would let their kids drink nothing! You'd have to be grown before you ever got to drink anything like that. They'd set their wine in the kitchen cabinets. They'd tell their kids not to bother it and they didn't. They told the kids what to do in them days. Nowadays, the kids tell their parents what to do.

Wine's good for anybody, good to thin their blood. If you've got thick blood, a doctor will give you wine. He did my daughter in Atlanta. She'd get blood clots. Thick blood is what causes blood clots. By gosh, the doctor told her to get some wine and drink it. Said, "You drink you some wine along all the time." She did and she quit having those blood clots in her legs.

Me and a fellow by the name of Walden made elderberry wine up there at his house. He called me and told me the dadblamed wine was ready and to come up there—me and him would sample 'er out. I went up there and me and him got to drinking that blasted stuff, and I set around there until, I guess, eleven o'clock that night. When I got ready to start home, I was so drunk I couldn't find my dadblasted horse where I had him tied. Then when I did, I couldn't hardly get on 'im. I don't remember getting home.

I went in and took the globe off one of those ol' kerosene lamps and started to light it. (We didn't have electric lights then.) I dropped the globe and broke it. I went in another room and hunted another one, started to light it, and broke it, too. That woke my daddy up. He come in and hunted up a light and wanted to know what was the matter with me. He'd never seen me drunk. That was the first time. He didn't get mad at me. He didn't say nothing much to me. Just, "Now, Son, I want you to get in the bed," and he went and fixed my bed and put me in it. I got up the next morning and was so sick! I guess it was ten or fifteen years before I drunk anything else.

A few years back, I was at a fellow's place one evening and he had kegs settin' along this place one after the other. Me and him was setting talking and he said, "I want you to taste some of this wine." It seemed like he had every kind of wine you could think of. Well, I took a swallow out of this one and—boys!—it was good! Then I took some out of one of the others—it seemed like that one was a little better. I took a little sup out of this one and a little sup out of that one. By the time I got around, I had drunk a whole lot of wine. First thing I knowed, my head was going around and around. I guess I drunk a pint.

I made some homebrew one time, made a big bunch of it. There's a difference in wine and homebrew. It's more like liquor than anything else. It'll make you drunk, that stuff will!

I had a little cellar that I dug and I made some, but I didn't want my younguns to know nothing about it. I just made a little for myself, you know. And I put it out there in that cellar and that John boy of mine and that girl of mine, Betty—one Saturday I was gone, and they was at playing around—the first thing you know, they found it. And they drunk a half a gallon of that stuff—didn't know better—and they was drunk as cooters! Their mother didn't know what was the matter with them, but I knowed just as quick as I laid eyes on 'em what had happened! I went straight out there and looked—they drunk a way down there in that half-gallon can! I never did make any more of that homebrew!

I lived at Rabun Gap. I had a big ol' cellar out there, and I put that homebrew in that cellar. I mean a whole bunch of homebrew! And I give it away. People around used to make a whole lot of homebrew. They'd bottle it up and sell it in the bottle. It'd be agin' the law to fool with so people quit making it. I had some homebrew blow up on me. Canned it too quick and it just blew the top right off.

I could make it again. I believe it would come to me if I started to making it. You've got to get Blue Label [Ribbon] malted syrup from the store. It comes in cans. Just put it in there and mix it up good. Put you some sugar in there and that stuff will go to working. But you can smell it five miles. You can't make it without somebody knowing it. They can open the door where it's at and they can smell that nasty stuff. You can make wine and nobody can hardly smell it. You kindly keep it in a cool place and nobody won't hardly smell it at all. That homebrew—you can't hardly get by without somebody smelling it. If they come in the house and I had it working yonder in one of them rooms, they could smell that stuff. You can smell that homebrew a mile.

Some people cut up a few Irish potatoes to put in it. Slice them up when the brew is working off. (You have to work it off three or four times to have good homebrew.) Lord, have mercy, that'll give the awfullest headache you ever had in all your life. You can ask anybody that makes homebrew, if they put Irish potatoes in it, it'll bust your head. I don't know why, and they ain't nobody else that can tell you. It don't take but a drink or two to give you a headache. Your head will just pop nearly. I don't know what that Irish potato does to it. A lot of people put it in, but I never did but one time. I know it'll give you the headache. I've tried it.

A fellow that lived not too far from me brought me some one time when I was working out here on the golf course. (I fixed that golf course and stayed there three years.) He made some good homebrew. He come there one time and give me a drink of homebrew and that was as good a homebrew as I've ever drunk in my life. I guess I drunk a pretty-good-size glass full and it was good. A month or two after that, he came by there and he said, "Lawton, I've got some more good homebrew, and I decided to bring you a jar." He brought me a half a gallon. Well, I set it down and didn't drink any right then. I took it to the house, and took me a drink of it, and it wasn't no time until I took the headache. My head hurt and hurt. I took some aspirins and it didn't do it no good. I went to sleep and slept awhile, and it got better that night. The next day I didn't drink none. The next evening I come in from work and I took me another drink. And I took the durn headache again. Well, I knowed then what give me the headache.

The next day he come by and he said, "Lawton, ain't that homebrew a lot better than the other?"

I said, "No, it ain't by me."

He said, "Why?"

I said, "I take the headache ever' time."

He said, "That's because I put a few Irish potatoes in it and that'll cause you to have a headache." I don't know why they'd want to put Irish potatoes in it to give you a headache.

I made grape juice, too. Pick your grapes when they're good and ripe, wash 'em good, and put 'em in a canning jar and add hot water and a little sugar. You want to make sure you've got just enough sugar in it to make the juice sweet. The grapes set at the bottom of the can and when the juice starts coming out of them, those grapes go to coming to the top.

It don't take too many grapes to make it, but it's the best juice you ever drunk. There's no joke about it. That's good stuff! It's got the flavor of the grape. That's the easiest stuff made in the world. It ain't wine—it's just juice. It's never worked or anything. They ain't no alcohol to it. I'd rather have this than three Coca-Colas™. Instead of making tea, I'll pour me out a glass of that and drink it. I drink it a lot of times when I'm eating stuff.

Now, plain grape juice ain't as good as muscadine is. You take muscadine and they've got a flavor that just won't quit. You know how good they smell. You smell them along the road, you know. They make better juice than [other] grapes. That's just a good drink now. If somebody just wants a drink, they can get 'em a glass of that and put some ice in it and it is good stuff.

"Blackberry wine is good for the tummyache."

~MARY PITTS~

Mary Pitts was one of Foxfire's earliest supporters. Back in 1966, when those first students were learning about postal regulations and third-class bulk mailing, she was the postmistress at Rabun Gap. These days she enjoys crocheting intricate designs for bedspreads and tablecloths and making quilts for her children and grandchildren, and now even great-grandchildren! She has shared quilt patterns with us and is also known to Foxfire for her cooking. Several of her recipes are in The Foxfire Book of Appalachian Cookery. *(Her husband, Esco, was also a frequent Foxfire contact.)*

Mrs. Pitts is a petite, pretty lady who doesn't look or move like she is in her eighties. She grew up in Commerce, Georgia, in the foothills of the Appalachian mountains, about 1½ hours' drive from Rabun County.

I usually use the blue Concord grapes for my grape wine. Lots of years my grapes don't make, so I make more blackberry wine than I do grape wine. I make the blackberry wine in the summer during blackberry season. Summer for blackberries, fall for grapes.

The way I make wine, whether it's blackberry, grape, or whatever, is to put the fresh-picked berries in a 2-gallon jar. Add about 2 quarts of water to 2 gallons of berries and then add sugar. I use about 5 pounds of sugar in all. It takes 2 cups of sugar to each gallon of berries to make them work off, so I put in 4 cups of the sugar when I let the 2 gallons of berries work the

Mary Pitts

first time. (It takes a little more sugar for muscadines than it does for regular grapes.) Let them set for about two to three weeks until all the berries go down [finish bubbling]. It's pretty cool on my porch where the crock sits, but wine works off better in hot weather than in cold weather. After the two to three weeks, I crush the berries (or grapes) good and get all the juice out. I pour them through cheesecloth. You should get 2 gallons of juice out of the 2 gallons of berries (plus the water and sugar).

Measure the juice and pour it back into the crock and add 2 more cups of sugar. Then just tie the jar off with a cotton cloth.

In about a week, I pour the juice through a cheesecloth again to get any more scum off. I pour the juice back into the crock and add another cup of sugar. It works off some more. I usually do this two more times, about a week apart, adding a cup of sugar and stirring it good each time.

Then I strain the wine again to be sure it's clear, and then pour it into quart jars. Don't seal the jars. Don't put the caps on too tight. Tighten the cap and give it one turn back. The wine might work some more and spew over. It'll take it three months to age.

I usually have the wine ready just before Christmas so I'll have some for my cakes. I make it and leave it in the kitchen. We don't drink it. The kids'll come in sometime and they'll want to taste Granny's wine, you know. *Shew!* They can't stand it! Which is good! But I use it more in cookies and on my fruitcakes.

I make about 30 pounds of fruitcake every year. I make a big one (about an 8-pound cake in a stem pan) and send it to my daughter. The others I make in loaf pans. They're about 3 pounds each.

I really made up my own fruitcake recipe. I use a pound cake recipe for my cake part. And then I put in anything else I want. I do leave off 1 cup of sugar in the pound cake batter because the fruits will sweeten the cake enough.

1 cup Crisco	*3 cups sugar*
1 cup milk	*3 cups flour*
6 eggs	*¼ teaspoon salt*
Vanilla, lemon, and almond extracts	*¼ teaspoon baking powder*

I mix all that up together and it makes a big pound cake. I add coconut and black walnuts, pecans, raisins, dates, mixed fruits, candied pineapple, and cherries—just fill that pound cake batter full.

Grease your cake pans good. And then line your pans with paper cut from brown-paper bags. This keeps the cakes from burning. Cook the cakes about two hours at 350 degrees. After I take my cakes out of the oven, I set them on a board, leaving them in the pans for about fifteen minutes. Then I loosen the cakes from the pans (do not take the cakes out of the pans) and while they are still hot, I pour the wine on them. I pour about half a cup of wine on each loaf cake, and about three-fourths of a cup on that big stem cake. Soak 'em good in wine. Cover them with a cloth and set them back for three days. I put mine on the back porch, and when they get good and cold, and all the wine is soaked in and they're not soggy, I turn them out of the pans and peel the paper off. Then I take another half cup of wine and I pat it on. I take my hand and just wet it good and pat it on the back of the cake and all around. Then I wrap it up with waxed paper and aluminum foil. Now they're fixed and I just set them back. It's a lot of hard work.

Blackberry wine is good for the tummyache and it's a good cure for diarrhea, too. My mother used to keep it all the time. It only took a little—I'd say a ¼ of a cup. That would be a big dose for a kid.

We used to have a cider press. In the fall of the year, us kids had to pick up apples and wash them. If there were any bad ones, we had to pick them out, take them out and just use the good ones. Then we'd put them in the press. I never did run the press, but you had to screw it down some way from the top and the juice would come out down below in a container. Then Mother would strain that juice. We'd make 3 or 4 gallons of juice, then set the press back. We drank that until it began to get sharp. We used to make apple cider all the time. But you know, you set that cider back and it makes vinegar. So we always made our vinegar at home.

I also can blackberry juice. I've got a vine of blackberries in the garden and I get 8 or 10 quarts off of it every year. I put my berries in a pot with enough water to cover them. I put them on the stove and let them simmer until they just go to mush. Then I strain them, put my juice back on the stove, and let it come to a boil. Then I put it in quart jars and seal them. I use it during the wintertime to make jelly and to make juice pies—blackberry pies without seeds.

I don't make any *real* blackberry pies with the real berries—seeds and all. I just use the juice. I put my quart of juice in a pan and add a cup of sugar and a stick of butter, and let it come to a boil. Then I make up my biscuit dough, just like I was going to make biscuits. I roll it out thin and cut it in little squares and drop the squares in that boiling juice. The juice will boil up as the squares are dropped in. Then I set the pan in the stove and let the dough squares brown. The kids call it "blackberry dumplings."

"The taste of it is so good."

~ALBERT & ETHEL GREENWOOD~

ALBERT: Our nephew brought a bunch of grapes from South Carolina, both kinds—some red'n's and some old white ones. He wanted wine made out of the red ones and the white ones, too. There is a gallon of it sitting in the canning house now.

ETHEL: The year before there were the most grapes. A person could have all he wanted down there.

ALBERT: I bet I could have got 4 bushels down there. It is the only muscadine vine I ever saw in this part of the county. These here vines, they're all just a lot of overweight berries. They were under the leaves and they were soft plants. You don't want them too green—you want them ripe.

Muscadines are tame grapes. Now you need not fool with any white grapes 'cause they're too sweet—they're no good. You crush them up. You can put them in a pan or whatever you want to. I use a tater masher that you mash taters [potatoes] with. It works pretty good. You can make a gallon or you can make a peck or you can make a half-bushel. You crush your grapes and you put them in a jar—stone jar. You set them back, then you want to cover that up. You could put a little piece of cloth over that and tie it around there, 'cause they's some kind of little ol' gnats that'll swarm around. We call them drunkards.

You set that back and let it ferment. Put your jar in a warm place about three days and nights. But don't let it stay in there too long. Then take it out

Ethel & Albert Greenwood

and strain it. That gets all the dregs out of it. There'll be some that settles. The fine ones just go through the cloth. You drain it off. You don't have to strain it again. Most of that will settle in your jar. You'll have to have a pretty stout cloth, something like a flour sack. You don't get many of them anymore. You spread that over your container or whatever you're straining it in. Then you dip it out and just gather the cloth up and twist it until you get all of it out that you can.

Now you'll have to wash that cloth. Once in a while, it causes that pulp in those grapes to stick to it. The juice won't go through much. Just wash it out good. It won't have enough water on it to hurt anything.

You have two cups, 'cause you can't dip your wet cup in the sugar. [One cup is used for dipping the must (the fruit, water, and sugar mixture) out for straining—the other is for adding sugar.] It don't matter about the size of the cups.

I don't remember how much sugar I put in that last batch I made. It depends on what kind of grapes. If the grapes are good and ripe, you want to

Albert Greenwood

add as little as possible. After you strain it, you put in three parts juice and one part of sugar. You put in the sugar and juice and stir it in the jar—kinda dissolves it. You can taste of it and tell if it's sweet enough. Muscadine keeps more sour than jelly grapes. Now, I'll tell you, don't add a thing in the world to your sugar and juice.

ETHEL: We didn't put no water in it. A lot of people put a lot of water in it and that ruins it.

ALBERT: You don't add no water, no nothing. After you put 'em in the jar, you let 'em ferment. You let the wine set three or four weeks. [You cover it with] aluminum foil.

ETHEL: Or put something around the little neck.

ALBERT: You put a rubber band around it. There's a little ol' gnat that flies around there. They like wine. When it quits working, you can tell when it quits—them little bubbles stop coming up. Until then you can't bottle it up and shake it up in a fruit jar, because it creates a gas. It'd bust the can, if the lid don't blow off. It don't matter how long you leave it in the jar, it don't hurt it. I've heard that you could make wine out of other things. I tried to make some out of buckberry—those little wild black berries in the woods—and it never did get sour. It didn't. It didn't ferment at all. It wasn't no good. I just poured it out.

ETHEL: A whole gallon.

ALBERT: It was so sour—

ETHEL: It was just like vinegar.

ALBERT: Well, you see, I was just experimenting [using the signs to make wine]. Whenever the grapes get ripe are the only signs I use. I never did go much by the signs.

ETHEL: Only when he made that kraut.

ALBERT: Yeah, you'd better do that, because when me and Ethel made these last two jars of kraut here, we just made it when we got ready—and there was something that wasn't right.

ETHEL: That wild strawberry [wine]—that was the best stuff I ever tasted in my life.

ALBERT: *Wild* strawberry. Now, that stuff I made out of them tame ones, it wasn't good for nothing.

ETHEL: They were too ripe.

ALBERT: They were also mushy. I just thought that it'd be a pretty thing, but it wasn't. If you could ever get some wild strawberries and make some, make it on the same recipe [as grape wine]—that's the best I ever tasted.

ETHEL: That's one thing I would have made if we could have got any wild strawberries. I'd made a good run of that. That was the best I ever tasted.

ALBERT: The taste of it is so good.

ETHEL: We made it just for ourselves.

ALBERT: I make wine for medicine. I never sold a drop of it in my life.

ETHEL: Back when he didn't have no appetite, I tried to get him to take it in that glass about thirty minutes before breakfast, and it didn't help him very much. But since he's got out of the hospital, he doesn't need nothing for appetite. He eats like a pig.

ALBERT: Well, I'll tell you, this is good for a sick stomach—a little of it every morning, if you feel dull.

"Oh, it's delicious—but it's no 'toxication about it, now, no 'toxication."

~NORA GARLAND~

I can tell you how to make persimmon beer. Gather your persimmons when the frost is on 'em. They'd be bitter if you didn't work it while the frost was on 'em. Put 'em in your churn, or what you're gonna make it in. I used to use a 5-gallon churn. I'd fill it half full [of persimmons]. You pour some hot water over it and let 'em sit there until they get good and soft. Then you put some sugar and honey locusts in 'em. [Honey locusts are] great big long things that grow on honey locust trees. Them honey locusts, they look kinda black and bad, but they're nice. They got a lotta honey in 'em. There's one side of them locusts that's thick. Well, that's full of honey and that helps sweeten the beer. You can use the pure honey locusts [instead of sugar] if you can get enough. Just break 'em up and put 'em in with your persimmons. If you couldn't find honey locusts, I guess you could use just pure honey like you get in jars. You'd use about a pint, I guess, but them locusts give it a good taste. Let that stay in there till it works. And then, when you take the persimmons out, you put some more sugar in and let it work.

See about it every once in a while. Stir it up and see how it's a'tastin'. I guess you can let it set a couple days. If you let it set too long, it might get hard [alcoholic]. [Next] strain your beer and put it in your containers or what you're gonna put it in. Let it get right hot and put it in your cans and seal it just like tomato or grape juice or anything else. It's just sweet enough to be good. Oh, it's delicious—but it's no 'toxication about it, now, no 'toxication.

Nora Garland

'Twon't make you drunk. They's no kick to it, no way. Mother used to make it and we'd serve it at the table. We'd get a glass apiece, y'know. I used to make it and I'd give it to the children at Christmas, the boys at Christmas.

We've made apple cider many times. We put it in gallon jugs and set it up and drunk it when we wanted it. We crushed the apples—we had a cider mill—and this crushed the apples. We washed the apples and put 'em in and turned the crank. The juice would all come out of the apples. That was cider. But, if you wanted it hard or anything, put some sugar in it and let it sit for a few days. Don't let it get too hard, it'll make you drunk!

[For apple juice,] you just cook your apples. Now the peeling on apples makes better juice [and] makes better jelly. Cook 'em, and strain your juice and can it, just like you'll can tomatoes or anything else.

I make grape juice all the time, when I can get the grapes. You just cook your grapes and strain your juice and put the juice in cans. You process it—cook it about ten minutes. You sweeten that when you drink it. You just pour it out in your glass and you can put sugar in it. I've got two rooms upstairs and I've got a big high shelf up there that I set my stuff on—my persimmon beer, my tomato juice, and my grape juice.

Blackberry makes good juice, too. I make my pies with the juice. I don't use the blackberries. I just pour it in my pan and make my pie. I guess I might make a pie different from anybody else, but I'll take one cup of flour and one stick of butter, and I take my hand and work that up till it's just as like meal, just as fine as it can be. Well, when my juice gets to boilin', I put that in there and I keep back enough [dough] to make a top crust on the pie and set it in the stove.

I went to a place for Christmas—I was invited for supper and a man came out with little glasses of wine, and I thought that was the best stuff, honestly, I ever put in my mouth. Shannon said, "This is wine—this is shore enough wine." And I handed it back to her and I said, "I don't want it. I drink neither wine nor strong drink."

Wine is good as a remedy [for] most anything. Law! It's good for your stomach! Nothing's better for your stomach than wine. Any kind of wine. Every day my girl would come over to the house and say, "I never had the stomachache so bad in my life." I knew right then she wanted a glass of wine. I'd go and get her 'bout a half a glass of wine. She was all right. It wasn't anything—she just wanted that wine.

"It was really good, but we didn't get much of it."

~CHRISTINE WIGINGTON~

After a talk to a ladies' church group in Salem, South Carolina, someone there mentioned a lively, eighty-three-year-old woman who plays the guitar and vividly remembers moving from the North Carolina mountains to Georgia's Piedmont region in a covered wagon. She sounded interesting, so several students went back to Salem, about an hour's drive from Rabun County, to interview Mrs. Christine Wigington for the first time.

Mrs. Wigington still lives in the white, one-story house built by her grandfather when she was very small. Behind the house, she keeps a garden grown high with corn, okra, and tomatoes, which she tends to with almost no help. She also enjoys crocheting, knitting, embroidering, and quilting, and she regularly attends her church group meetings on Tuesdays. It is not unusual to find Mrs. Wigington staying up until two o'clock in the morning in order to finish a book—she says she has "read nearly every book in the library." On a follow-up visit, we discovered that she is also interested in winemaking and can still remember some of her father's recipes.

I remember my father would gather the persimmons and locusts and we'd usually make persimmon beer—Mama would. The honey locusts, like we have down here, grow in the woods. When they just start falling, they've got that—we used to call it honey—in 'em. We'd put the whole thing in there. If you wait too long [to gather the locusts], there's a little worm that

"It was really good, but we didn't get much of it."

Christine Wigington

gets in there. [We'd put layers of locust and layers of ripe persimmons] in what we call a churn jar—a crock, I believe they call it—was one that holds about 4 or 5 gallons. [We'd pour hot water in] and usually turn a plate down, bottom side up, on the churn and put a cloth over it. I don't think the persimmon beer would ferment. You just leave it in there long enough till it would get the flavor. Persimmon beer is more like a cider, only it was better.

My daddy used to make what he called peach brandy, too.* You peel and slice peaches, put 'em in a half-gallon fruit jar, and put sugar on 'em 'bout like you'd sweeten 'em to eat. And then just put a lid on that, very light, because when you ferment it, it'll blow up [if the lid is tight]. When it would ferment and quit bubbling, it was ready to drink. Then he'd strain it out. It was really good, but we didn't get much of it. My daddy drank most of it!

[My son] Max—I think it was his first attempt to make blackberry wine—put it in a churn jar, not a big one, and he set it back in a bathroom that they wasn't using. He didn't know whether you put one or two cakes of yeast in it, so to be safe, he put two. He didn't notice it was fermenting, and he thought he'd move it into the kitchen to strain it. Well, he got about halfway into the kitchen and the thing blew up! He said there was blackberries on the ceiling, all over him, and everywhere else!

* In the recipe section, this appears as Christine Wigington's Recipe for Peach Wine.

"Throw the medicine out and give him the wine!"

~GRANNY [LYNDALL] TOOTHMAN~

Elderberry makes one of the best wines of anything. The elderberries usually get ripe about the last of September, just before frost. You gather the berries in the big bunches, wash them if they are dusty, and then strip the small berries off the bunches and mash them till they are mushy. (You don't have to be real careful about stripping them. A few small stems won't hurt.) Use a stone jar to ferment the wine in, and cover it with a clean cloth so it can get air yeast.

We just put in about 3 pounds of sugar to the gallon of berries. I'd put about a pound to the gallon of berries for the first three days. Then strain it through a thin cloth—a cheesecloth is good. Then put the rest of the sugar in and let it run off a second time so you get a whole lot stronger wine. Let it set till it quits bubbling.

When it stops bubbling, you can put it in your jars and put it away in a cellar where you don't bother it for six months.

Some people put a slice of white bread on top of the mashed berries. As the pulp comes to the top, it will hold the bread up, and on that bread they put a cake of Fleischmann's Yeast™ and leave it for three days. They'd have to take it off carefully and not let the yeast or the bread go down in the juice. My mother never used any yeast—just the whole juice, not watered down. It's beautiful! The prettiest color of wine, a real deep cardinal.

My mother had some of this wine one time when my father was sick.

Granny Toothman

The doctor came and asked her for something to give father to take the medicine in. Mother brought out some elderberry wine. The doctor drank some and said, "Throw the medicine out and give him the wine!"

You can make blackberry wine this same way. I have also made rhubarb wine like this. Cut the rhubarb in small pieces and put all the sugar on top of it, and the sugar will draw the juice from the rhubarb. When I was a youngster, the air was pure and the spring water pure, but I don't know whether anything works the same anymore. But we can always try!

I guess the dandelion wine was sort of a different thing, too. From the time I was six years old on, it was all right to have a little glass of wine if our family had made it ourselves. About a year ago, I made some dandelion wine the same old way and it turned out fairly well. You get about a gallon of the yellow blossoms—pick them right at the top of the stem—and you take 2 gallons of boiling water and pour that over the blossoms and add 3 pounds of sugar and a sliced lemon and 2 sliced oranges, peeling and all. Have all this in a big stone crock, and leave it three days. Then you strain the blossoms and everything out of it and add 2 or 3 pounds of sugar and let it sit at least nine days in a warm place. Keep a light, porous cloth on top, so that the air can go through so it can gather that air yeast. By that time, it's just about quit going up and down [working], and then you strain it off again and put it in your bottles. Don't cork them too tight 'cause you might have an explosion! You take it and set that back in the cellar and don't even remember it's there until Christmas. You make it in the spring, so by Christmas it's been in there about six months or more, and it's good. It's pretty strong, too!

The first time I ever drank much of it, it really gave me a belt. I was about fifteen, and a cousin of mine had slipped and made a big jar of it, and he had it back in the hills in a cold spring. We were having dinner there that evening and he asked if we'd like a glass of that wine. Of course, all of us wanted one, but I didn't know how powerful it was. It tasted like real bubbly good punch. It was just before dinner, and I was very hungry and that just tasted like real good punch. I sat there and in about half an hour that big glass of wine he gave me was all gone. And after it was all gone, why, I started to get up, but I was just a little juberous [sic] and I didn't think I could make it! So I sat real still. I had drunk wine ever since I was a child, but that was the first time I had had it to hit me. The empty stomach and the high potency of the wine did the work. So anyway, I sat there, and my cousin's wife was putting the dinner on the table. She said, "I want you to sit over here." Instead of getting up and going over, I took my chair and scooted it over to the table and ate my dinner. After I ate my dinner, of course, that took the edge off of it and I was all right, but that was my first experience with really getting high. And that's about the only one!

We also made strawberry wine. We had loads and loads of wild strawberries, and every spring I picked gallons of them and Mother would put sugar on top of the berries and the juice would raise up. She didn't want that juice in her preserves anyway. She wanted her preserves kind of dry. So she always poured this juice out into the big jar, and, of course, she already had the sugar in it. You didn't know how much sugar really was in this juice, but if you set it in a moist temperature in the cellar and forgot about it and let it do its own thing, sometimes it made real good wine. She didn't seal it until maybe in the fall, and then she would look at it and taste it. Once in a while, if the season and the weather weren't exactly right, it didn't work, and once in a while, it would go to vinegar. But the usual thing was we had a gallon or so of just delicious strawberry wine out of the pure juice, and it was a dear and beautiful bright red wine color. I know even when I was very small, my dad used that for medicine. He always said that the Bible said that a little wine was good for your stomach, and when we would get the stomachache, Dad would always go and get us a little glass of this strawberry wine and give it to us. And if we were really sick, it *did* help. If we weren't really sick, I guess it helped, too!

One of the oldest drinks in the world is mead. If you have extra honey, you might try this. It is very simple—tastes a little like homebrew. You will need 4 or 5 pounds of honey to a gallon of water. Have the water hot and mix the honey in it so the honey is dissolved. (It doesn't have to be strained honey.) Put it in a stone jar. Dissolve a cake of wine yeast and add to the honey mixture. Cover with a thin cloth and put the jar in a dark cellar. Let it set six weeks to two months. Then see about it, and if it is settled down (through working), strain it and bottle. Sugar can be used instead of all honey, but real mead is just water and honey.

"The lid was raising up and down, just as regular as you've ever seen."

~CLARENCE & ALMA LUSK~

Clarence Lusk met us at the front door of his white, one-story house in Salem, South Carolina, with a grin. As he ushered us into an enclosed porch, we noticed the healthy plants that lined the window sills and the basket ferns that hung from the ceiling. Several comfortable chairs took up the floor and sunshine flooded the room. Mr. Lusk motioned for us to sit down and we made ourselves at home. Soon, the smell of sourdough bread drifted out from the kitchen and Mrs. Lusk appeared in the doorway. As Clarence talked about making corncob wine, Alma brought us iced tea and cake.

CLARENCE: I make corncob wine in the summertime when the corn gets ripe. I use yellow corn in mine, but it doesn't matter what type you use. First, shear the fresh corn off the cob. Then just use whatever is left on the cob. Pack the cobs in a 3-gallon churn. Fill the churn almost to the top with the cobs. Pour in enough water to cover the cobs, but leave about three or four inches at the top so it won't run over.

I let it stand about eight or nine days, depending on how hot the weather is. You will know when it is fermented because it will smell soured. It smells like corn beer. Don't let it stand over nine days or it will get too sour. Then take the cobs out and strain all the juice off through a little cloth. Get all of the sediments out of it. It will look kind of milky.

When it is fermented, I have a gallon of juice. I then wash my churn

Alma & Clarence Lusk

out and pour the juice right back in it, and add 3 pounds of sugar to a gallon of juice. (You need to add that much sugar because that is part of the fermenting process. If you don't, it's likely to taste more like vinegar than wine.) I put one little package of Fleischmann's Yeast™ in a cup and dissolve it and pour that into the churn. Put the yeast in the juice and let that stand for about ten more days. After ten days, it ought to begin to taste like wine. It works twice, once with the cobs in there and a second time when you put your sugar and yeast in it. It takes about eighteen days to make. The longer you let it sit, the sharper it gets.

If you want the wine to be stronger (more alcoholic), then go back and pour about 1½ pounds more sugar in it and let it work nine or ten more days. It will also taste sweeter. But you never add more water. What the wine is made of is what controls its sweetness or tartness. Corncob will not be as sweet as grape.

Let me give you an example of what happens when the wine starts making. I made some wine one time and set it on the sink. I was sitting here one day and I heard something going, "thump, thump." I kept looking around and I got to thinking the sink was leaking. I got up and started watching that jug. The lid was raising up and down, just as regular as you've ever seen.

When you bottle your wine up, after you pour it up and put your lids on, tighten them down just enough to stay on there. If you tighten the lids on too tight, the bottles will blow up.

Scuppernong grapes ripen in the middle of September. To make scuppernong wine, you fill up a 3-gallon jar full of grapes, leaving enough room at the top so they won't boil over. You mash them up, burst every one of them. I generally do that with my hands. Then pour a little water over them until they are just floating. Not a great big pile of water, now. If you do, the wine will be too weak. Let it stand about eight or nine days, according to how hot the weather is. Then you strain that out. It's a little harder to strain than the corncob on account of the pulp. I take a screen wire and let the juice run through. I empty the pulp and keep pouring until I get the juice I need.

Measure that juice, put 3 pounds of sugar per gallon, and add a packet of yeast. Cover the jar up good to keep the flies and gnats from getting in there. It tastes like wine in ten days, but the longer you let it sit, the better it is. Don't ever close it up tight for a year or so, because it still has a tendency to work a little bit, and it will explode if you put it in a glass jar and tighten the lid.

You make blackberry wine the same way as scuppernong, but the berries are just easier to mash up.

ALMA: I had some apple, grape, peach, and plum juices that I hadn't used. I hated to throw them out so I gave them to Clarence to make wine out of. He mixed all the juices together and it was really good. That was the best wine he had ever made. You can make wine out of any fruit.

My doctor is from the lower part of the state. He said when he was a boy, his daddy had a smokehouse and he used to make big barrels of wine in that smokehouse. He used to keep something fermenting all the season. The doctor said he and his brother loved it when they were sent into the smokehouse after something. They would take them a quill and stick it down in those barrels and they would suck the wine out of there.

My mother would make vinegar. She'd take bee comb and squeeze the honey out of the comb. She'd put that comb in a jar and pour water over that until the water just come over the comb. Let it sit there, and that would turn into vinegar.

31

"My daddy used to make whiskey in a still out in the woods."

~IRENE RAMEY~

I've made blackberry, apple, tomato, and plum juice. Most of them are for making jelly, some are to drink. Blackberry juice is real good. I use it to make jelly or pies. Sometimes people would take it for medicine, for things like diarrhea.

Tomato juice is just actually a good drink, especially when you have a cold. A lot of people like to put salt in it and drink it for breakfast. My daddy liked it like that—when there was a little bit of salt and sugar in it. We used to make tomato gravy. I'd put the tomato juice in a pot, with a little bit of flour, sweet milk, and cook it until it gets thick. Then, put it over hot biscuits. It's good!

Plum juice is good to make jelly out of. I don't know whether it would be good to drink or not, but it does make good jelly.

And then there's apple juice. I make jelly out of that. I make apple juice and peach juice the same way. You don't have to peel them beforehand, but you can. Just wash it, cut it up, cut the core out and clean it up. Then put barely enough water to cover up the apples or peaches. Cook it until it's tender and set it out to cool so you can strain it out.

For berries, you wash them and cook them the same way. Just cook them until they're mushy and soft. To strain them, I put them in a cloth bag so I can squeeze the juice out. Then, I run that through a colander to be sure the seeds are all out. Of course, you throw the pummy [seeds, etc.]

Clayton & Irene Ramey

away. Then, you've got your juice. If it's something I'm going to drink, I put sugar in it, but if I'm going to make jelly, I don't. You can can the juice to use later or to drink, or make wine out of. Well, I don't know how to make wine. I ain't never got that far yet! People used to make a lot of wine and brandy. I've tasted some before, but I don't like anything much that tastes like it's fermented alcohol. But a lot of people does.

My daddy used to make whiskey in a still in the woods, when I was a little girl. There was four of us girls and when my brother came along Daddy said, "No more of that. I've got by with my girls, but I can't do this with my little boy, so I've got to just quit." And he did—he quit. He didn't have anything to do with it anymore. His singing took his time. That's what he enjoyed was his singing.

People used to always have grapes. They'd be Concord grapes or wild muscadines. A lot of people love muscadine juice! When we lived at Rabun Gap on the school farm, I had—oh, I don't know—cans and cans of it. Everybody up there found out I had it and they came and wanted some of it to drink. So I gave *several* cans of it away to people who wanted to drink it.

I have, lots of times, took grapes and muscadines and mashed them out and took the pummy part of it, the inside part, and made cakes. Then, I'd take the outside part, and make preserves. They're something good! Just mash your grapes out.

[Also] take the inside to make jelly. Take that pummy and cook it until it's tender. Then put sugar in it and cook it down. I don't think I've made any since the year your Daddy and Mother got married [referring to student Donna Ramey's parents—Mrs. Ramey is Donna's grandmother]. They went down and got me a peck bucket full. I sat down and mashed them out and made jelly and preserves out of it. It was a lot of work, but it paid off.

You know what dried fruit is, don't you? You can dry the peeling of an apple, pack it down in a churn, and pour hot water over it to make what we called apple beer. You have to put sugar in with it, too. It was really just a soft drink. If you were real tired, it'd help you rest. What's real good to mix it with is wild locust [referring to the ripened seed pods of locust trees].

Another thing we used to have is what they call California beer seeds. They were just seeds that you could order. You could put them in a churn, put water over them, let them sit so many days, and then have beer. Then, you could take the seeds out and put them in the sunshine. They'd dry out and you could use them again, over and over. Uncle John used to order them. He said he drank it for arthritis. It's about like apple juice. It wasn't alcoholic—it was just a drink.

We used to make our own vinegar from apples, which we don't do today. To make it you have to take your apples and grind them out like a cider, which is really what it is, then set it back to let it ferment and make your vinegar. Mother used to make vinegar pies and they were good. They had a tangy taste like vinegar, but they had a good taste too, kinda like rhubarb.

Rhubarb grows in your garden. It has big old green leaves and a big ol' stem. You cook the stem part. You cut it up and cook it, and by the time it gets hot, it's just all to pieces. It takes a lot of sugar to sweeten it. Then you just make a pie out of it like you would any other. It makes a good pie. We love it just cooked. Just cook it and eat it with hot biscuits. I have froze some and made jam out of it. I've got plenty of it!

[Talking about fruits and juices reminded Mrs. Ramey of other beverages that she remembers, such as teas.]

We used to make what you call spicewood tea. It was something like the tea we have today, but I called it homemade tea. It was a bush* that growed way out in the woods along creek banks. People would gather it and boil it to make tea. A lot of times we would drink it with supper. People would say that it made them sleep good. We used to have a bush right out there at the barn. There was many a batch of tea made off that thing! It's gone now—somebody cut it down.

I've never made any sassafras tea, but I've heard people talk about drinking it. I think it had some form of healing power. It would settle the nerves and other things like that—make them sleep. It was more what you call an herbal tea, I guess.

Comfrey is also an herbal tea, and I love it! I buy it at the health food store. You just boil it and sweeten it like you would any other tea.

---

* Most likely the native "spicebush" variety in the Calycanthus genus.

"You don't want to sample it too soon."

~MINNIE & ERVIN TAYLOR~

MINNIE: Back when we lived in Clairmont, Delaware, everyone made [homebrew] and bottled it up. My husband made it all the time. I didn't [drink it] because I didn't like the taste of it. The beer they have now, I don't like the taste of. These men drink it and a lot of these women drink it, too. Boys, I don't want none.

ERVIN: That was during prohibition days. You couldn't buy any hard liquor. Of course, that was before my time.

MINNIE: Lord, they've made homebrew ever since I can remember. Up north, everybody made it, nearly. Made it and bottled it up. I don't think it has to be made any certain time of the year. If you made pickled beans the wrong time of the year, they'll be soft and slick and they ain't no 'count. But they made homebrew anytime they wanted to. We used to make it all the time, but, Lord, it's been such a long time since I've made any. They made some down here around Wiley [Georgia]. They bottled it up before it got ready and it blowed the top off the pint can. I said if you were going to take a drank and it blowed up, you would be in for it.

ERVIN: The way I make homebrew, I put it in a 5-gallon churn that is just about half full of hot water, about up to where the handle is on that one. Then put 5 pounds of sugar to start with, [a large box of raisins], and a quart can of Blue Ribbon malt. You can buy the malt in stores. Put two packs of yeast in there. That's to start it to working faster. When it works off, it eats

Minnie Taylor

those raisins up and you don't have to strain those raisins out. You can cut up an Irish potato in it to give the brew a little more power. It gives it some strength. Then I'd let that work. If you wanted to double the power, you would let it work off and then add 5 more pounds of sugar. That doubles the strength. In this kind of [cool] weather it would take ten days [to work off]. When it stops bubbling, it's worked off. Like I said, if you wanted to double the strength, you would put 5 more pounds of sugar and let it work off.

You don't want to sample it too soon. If you do, you'll know about it. You'll really know about it! What it is, is homemade beer. My mother never would know what was in there in that utility room. I used to make homebrew in there. I had it in there until it got worked off and I got ready to drink it.

MINNIE: My aunt used to make wine. I stayed out there with her years ago. Doctor Fowler told her to make some, or get somebody to make her some blackberry wine—some homemade, not this you buy. He told her to take a spoonful every morning or at night, so she would eat good. She made some out there with my churns. Ervin picked the blackberries, then she made about 2 gallons of wine. She took 2 gallons of berries and put so much water, yeast, and sugar in it. [The amount of sugar used] was according to how many berries she had. If the berries are pretty sour, I guess you would have to put a pretty good bit of sugar. It's the same as what you would do if you were making homebrew. I guess that's the way you would do it. She put her berries, sugar, and yeast in a churn and added warm water. I don't know of anything else she would add, but we didn't put in anything that would give it a kick.

The wine would work off—you just give it time. You put that yeast in there and it will work off. You would keep a cloth tied over the churn to where nothing can get in it. [While it's working off] you can set it out on the porch or anywhere and let it go. By looking and listening, you can tell [that it has quit bubbling], but let it shore stay long enough until it's quit. If you bottled it up before it got done working, it would blow the top off of the jar! You make wine like you would pickled beans—when you make them you can tell when they get ready.

[Strain the wine with] something like a thin flour sack. Now, they don't have no flour sacks, but I used to use some old, thin curtains. You want that thin kind so the wine will go through—like you would strain jelly. After she got it fixed, she would put it up in jugs, cans, or something. You can put it in half-gallon jars or whatever you want to, but my aunt put hers in a jug. You could set the wine anywhere. Just set it in a place where it's cool.

This wine, it tastes pretty good, but I didn't want to drink much of it because I was a'feared I'd be gettin' to want to drink it all the time. I didn't want to start drinkin' it like some of these men does, so I just barely tasted of it. It was good!

I used to can grape juice. Just take about 2 cupsful of grapes, wash 'em and put 'em in a half a gallon glass jar. Pour boilin' water in on 'em and put about a cupful [of sugar] in. Put your lid on it and that water will seal it. It would make something to drink!

"If it's still a'bubbling and a'popping, you'll not fool with it."

~GROVER WEBB~

The only kinds of wine I've ever made are grape wine, rhubarb, and blackberry. You make rhubarb wine just like you make grape wine, but it don't take as long. You pick your rhubarb and skin it down, take the outside skin off of it. Then you cut it up real good and fine. If you've got a 5-gallon jar, you want to put the rhubarb in that. You want half-a-gallon water to every gallon of rhubarb. Then that rhubarb will make a lot of water. You put about 5 pound of sugar in it to start with and add a yeast cake or two. That starts it working. Then you let it work for seven days. It will quit working in seven days, and you take the rhubarb out and do away with that. Strain the juice through a [cheesecloth] strainer and put it right back in the jar. Sweeten it down again with 5 more pound of sugar and let that set for seven more days. Takes about fourteen days to make it. It's got full strength to it. It's *full* strength, too!

Then when it's done, put it in the refrigerator and let it get good and cold. Rhubarb wine will be a yellowish color. The longer you keep it, the better it gets. It's high!

You work your grapes the same way you work your rhubarb, but that rhubarb is naturally stronger than the grape. You want to pick your grapes when they are good and ripe. Then you mash your grapes. You put a gallon of grapes in the churn and mash them up good. You add a half-gallon of water to every gallon of grapes until your jar is filled up. Then you sweeten

Grover & Lucy Webb

them down just like you do the rhubarb. Say you gotta 5-gallon jar, you put 5 pound of sugar in that and start it that way and let it work. You can put you a yeast cake or two in there. That starts them working good! It takes longer to work grapes than it does rhubarb. You let that work as long as it'll work. You can raise your lid and look at it. If it's still a'bubbling and a'popping, you'll not fool with it. Just leave it alone. It'll finally quit bubbling. When it quits, you take it out and strain it just like you do the rhubarb. Mash your cheesecloth together and get all the juice out that way. Then you clean your jar good and pour your juice back in there. Then you sweeten it back just like you do the rhubarb. Put 5 more pound in it. That's 10 pound. That juice will start working again with that sugar. It'll work on and on. As long as it's a'working, every now and then you need to add a little sugar to it, about a pound or 2 pound. You don't want to put too much more. Then you let it work right on like that. If it's still working, you want to leave it working just as long as it will. When it quits bubbling and popping, it's made.

When you get that all worked off, you can strain it out again through a cheesecloth 'cause there'll be a lot of the grape pulp that went through the strainer the first time. When you strain it back again, it comes up clear, and it'll be a reddish color. Put it in jars. A lot of times there'll be a little settling in the bottom, but your top will be just as pretty and clear.

I usually make my wine around August when the grapes come in. The hotter the weather, the better it works. 'Course you can make it any time. You can buy these here California white grapes in the store and make wine out of them.

I don't like any kind of wine much. I used to like that rhubarb. That rhubarb is fiery. It's kind of high-powered. And the grape is, too, if you work it and make it real strong. It just takes a long time to make it.

Grapes, rhubarb, elderberries, blackberries—you can even make peach wine. Any kind of stuff like that you can make wine out of. Blackberries make good wine. It's the best kind of wine there is. I've made blackberry wine—made it just the same as the grape wine. It takes the blackberry about the same amount of time as the grapes to work, but you don't have to mash the blackberries up. There's a lot of people who use that wine in cakes. I don't know how much they put in it. They used to make what they called wine cakes. They'd bake a cake and then pour wine over it. They'd set it back and let it soak in. When you eat that thing, it's got that taste of wine in it. It's just a good taste. I've got a boy—his wife makes it, and I've eat some of theirs and that cake's real good, too.

"You can make wine out of anything but a rock!"

~JOHN & MARGARET BULGIN~

John and Margaret Bulgin are natives of Franklin, North Carolina, and are longtime friends of Foxfire. In his early eighties, Mr. Bulgin is a blacksmith who still runs a shop located behind his house. Mrs. Bulgin is in her early seventies and also stays busy helping run the farm. Their beautiful, modern home is located on a hill on the outskirts of Franklin and is surrounded by pasture. A barn sits in the back of the house, next to Mr. Bulgin's shop, and several birdhouses are situated on the front lawn. One of Mr. Bulgin's many interests is winemaking and, as we discovered, his specialty is rhubarb wine.

JOHN: You can make wine any time of the year. The grapes arrive [ripen] in August. But you can start making rhubarb as soon as it starts coming out. There's all kinds of wine: potato, carrot wine, and parsnip wine. I made some one time out of tomatoes. It had a pretty good taste. You can make wine out of anything but a rock!

I take just the stalk [of the rhubarb] and chop it up. To a gallon of chopped rhubarb, put a gallon of warm water and about 2 pounds of sugar. (And I don't put quite that much every time.) I don't know the exact amount. Rhubarb is very tart. You just don't want to get the wine too sweet. I use about a 5-gallon jug, and I put about 10 pounds of sugar to a 5-gallon jug of rhubarb. Of course, you can't fill the jug full because it'll begin to work, and [bubble] over. I sometimes use yeast to help the wine work. For about 5

Margaret Bulgin

gallons, I use one package of Fleischmann's™. You put the yeast in just before you put the cornmeal on the top.

When you get your jar full, cap it off with cornmeal. Just cover the rhubarb good with the cornmeal. The cornmeal floats and then, of course, some will mix with in with the rhubarb. It doesn't matter how much you use because it'll all come out when you strain it. The cornmeal adds a little to the alcohol and it seals the air off.

Next, cover the jug up good with four or five plies of cheesecloth, and then put a board on top of that. I take a rubber band and put it around the neck of the jar and try to seal all the outside air off.

Let the rhubarb work from seven to nine days. You don't want to let it go over nine days before you get the pulp out because then it's beginning to get slick and the wine will be black looking. When it gets through working, it'll quit bubbling. You strain it and then you ought to press it. Rhubarb is hard to get all the juice out of, by just twisting it in a rag. You need to wring it through into another container or put it in a press. It's getting the pulp out that you have to be careful with.

After you strain it, add a little sugar to taste and let it work again. Put another cheesecloth over your jug or container to cover it. You want to stir it about every day and when it quits bubbling, cover it good and let it sit. Oh, it doesn't matter how long you let it sit—you want to be sure it's quit working. You don't want to blow the bottles up. Then you put it into bottles, and we just seal it up and put a cork in it. Cap it. You can find plenty of wine bottles. I store mine in gallon jugs and keep the jugs in a cool (but not *too* cool) place. You don't want them to sit out in the sun. I put mine in the can house. I start making it down there in the can room and I store it in the same place.

Last year I put up about 8 or 9 gallons. I made two crocks. It's according to how much rhubarb you've got and how many crocks you've got. The wine is good to drink if it's done right and has a proof to it and has a good flavor. You can get it too sweet or you can get it too dry.

You can make grape and blackberry wines about the same way, but you don't have to have as much sugar for grapes. We did make some grape wine last year. You've got to crush your grapes up and add a little water to it and let it work. Add about a gallon of water to a gallon of crushed berries. You can start out with 1½ pounds of sugar to a gallon of crushed grapes. After it's worked and after you strain it, then you taste it to see if it's real sour or not. If it is, I add a little more sugar. You don't strain it but once to get all the pulp and stuff out of it. After it quits working, just seal the crock off with a cloth and a board and let it sit until you get ready to bottle it.

Homebrew is made with Blue Ribbon malt and so much water. I haven't made it in years. It's more like beer. It's got a pretty good alcohol content. I just use it for drinking, just to get drunk on. You make it in a crock just like you would wine. And you have to cap it. I used to have a capper and I would get caps, you know, just like a Coca-Cola™ cap, and put the homebrew up in the old-fashioned Coca-Cola™ bottles.

One time I was going by the instructions of this ol' guy and he told me my homebrew was ready to bottle. I bottled it up and put it down in the basement. (This was in the old house we tore down.) I just bottled it and corked it—capped it up too soon. It blew up! Heck, I was afraid to go down there!—glass a'flying everywhere and sticking in the floor. That homebrew will blow up!

MARGARET: I never put wine in fruitcakes as I'm making them. I have put a cloth over a fruitcake and dribbled some wine on it just to keep it moist. And then you get a little bit of the taste from it, too. Peach brandy

John Bulgin

is good for that. We don't make peach brandy. I have to buy that. I've made about five fruitcakes this year. I usually make them around Christmastime, through the holidays.

I sometimes can grape juice and blackberry juice to make jelly out of later on. I add just enough water to cover the grapes or berries, and then simmer them in a large gallon or gallon-and-a-half pot, until they are soft. Then I strain the juice out, discarding the pulp, and heat the juice again. Then I put it in jars and it will seal. Then I can use that canned juice to make my jelly anytime.

When I make the jelly, I add sugar to the juice and use Sure-Jell™, just following the instructions on the package. If you don't want to use Sure-Jell™, use a cup of sugar for each cup of juice. I store the jelly in pint jars and usually melt paraffin [wax] to pour over the top of the jelly to seal it. This keeps the jelly from molding.

"Work that off about twice and it'll make you slap your granny."

~MELVIN TAYLOR~

That twenty-four-hour cocktail will make you talk to yourself if you drink too much of it. It makes an awful good drink. Of course, you can't start drinking that stuff like you was drinking branch water. If you do, the first thing you know, your legs'll get wobbly under you. You have to hold on to something. That stuff is all right!

I think Casey Jones is the one that told me about it. That's been twenty-something years ago that I heard about it. I haven't made any of it in a long time.

I'll tell you the ingredients that go in it. You get a half-a-gallon of the meanest moonshine liquor you can find and put it in a 5-gallon churn. Put a half-a-gallon of water in it. Get you 2 dozen oranges, cut 'em open, and squeeze 'em in the churn. Throw the hull and all in it. Cut a dozen lemons, squeeze them out, and throw them in there, and do 3 grapefruits the same way. You have to squeeze every bit of fruit in there. Put all that in the churn and add 3 teacupsful of sugar to it. Stir it all up good, then you let it set twenty-four hours, and she's ready. You can set it anywhere. You get about 6 quarts. It's a good drink, man! You put some ice in a glass and put a little salt in that, stir that up, and boy, that's good stuff. It'll make you talk to your granny! You'll enjoy it!

The last time I made it, I made a double batch for a Christmas party. You can make all you want—you just double everything. I used a gallon of

Melvin Taylor

moonshine. As I squeezed [the fruit] out, I put some in my mouth. By the time I got through, I was drunk. I fell off the porch! I throwed the pummies out back where [my neighbor's] cattle was. They was out there eating them and, in a few minutes, one of them old cows bawled about twice an' come this way just a'flying! They drank it all up that night when I had the party. I had to go after something else. Now that's good stuff!

I've made homebrew, too. Get you a can of Blue Ribbon malt syrup and 5 pound of sugar and put that in water in a 5-gallon churn. It's all right to put some grapes or raisins in there with it. Cut up 3 or 4 Irish potatoes and put them in there if you really want to make it stout. (The potatoes have got a high alcohol content.) Work that off about twice and it'll make you slap your granny.

You've got to let it work off a pretty good while and, if you want to bottle it up, you better make sure it's all worked off. I capped some one time, and that night I never heard the like out of the can house. It busted the bottles and blowed the caps off of 'em. It wasn't worked off. After it's bottled, make sure you don't drink it before it gets ready. If you do, it'll put you to going to the woods!

[Melvin also said that it would be all right if the homebrew is worked off only once. If you want to work it off twice, more sugar must be added. As Melvin said, "That will just make it twice as stout."]

"It's almost like it's boiling—bluba, bluba, bluba."

~MINYARD CONNER~

Let's see... I moved out here in '36 and that's when I quit making wine. I learnt from the old people. My parents didn't make any wine that I know of.

You use the fruit—whatever kind you're using, grind it up. You know, let the juices run, and you put it into a barrel and let it work. It's almost like it's boiling—bluba, bluba, bluba. About the time it quits blubbing, just take it out and strain it. Then it's just like fruit tonic, except after a little while it'll be just like the fruit. It'll be just a mild wine.

You have to [separate the seeds from the fruit]. You can get nearly all the seeds. You can mash them out or take them out with your hands when they get good and ripe. Now, for grapes, you don't separate the seeds. Anything that has little seeds in it, you can let them go through.

Use a wooden barrel—oak barrel. You can use a 50-gallon barrel, a 30-gallon barrel, or a 10-gallon barrel. I never did use less than a 10-gallon barrel.

The amount of grapes I'd use would be accordin' to how much I could pack in a 10-gallon barrel. It wouldn't hold over a bushel, would it? The least amount of water you can put in, the better.

Now, if you want to get drunk and bat your eyes real good, I'd let it work off once and then sweeten it. To make it real stout, I'd put enough sugar in it to make it good and sweet. When you put the sugar in it, that

Minyard Conner

gives it twice as much alcohol. If you have a 8- or 10-gallon barrel, you'd maybe put in nearly a pound. If you want it strong, add a half-pound to the gallon.

I didn't go by the signs, but I heard 'em talk about things like that. I never did try nothing like the more sugar you put in your wine or anything to work it harder and faster. Maybe putting a piece of yeast in the wine would make it stronger. Now you put the yeast in that to make it work. Kinda pep it up a little—make it work faster.

You'd put the barrel in a place where you could take care of it. Keep it in your cellar. Keep it kinda cool all the time. I kept mine in a dug-out place under this house. [Let it sit] accordin' to the weather: If it's hot, it'd work off quicker; if it's cold, it'll take it longer. [If it was hot] I'd say it would take maybe a week, maybe two weeks. When we thought it was ready, we'd taste of it.

If you want to keep the wine from turning to vinegar, you can take apple cider [and add it] to the wine. Put [the cider] on the stove and let it just start to boil. As it begins to foam up, you just take the foam off. It'd keep, like that. (I've worked many a gallon of cider where I was raised. We had a cider mill, you know. I learned how to make cider that had sour apples, some of them so sour that they would make your lips turn in! Some of them were good and sweet as honey.)

I've made nearly all kinds of wine. Just about name it, I've made it. You can make plum wine, grape wine, blackberry wine, and elderberry wine.

I never use wine to cook with. I use it to drink. They claim it is good for diarrhea. If you got sick, it'd help you just like eatin' some apples or grapes. Something like that was good for you.

"Wild cherries make good wine."

~CARLTON ENGLISH~

I've made a lot of wine—made it off and on all my life. I hoped to [make some this year]. If the sun had been shinin', I was gonna go pick some berries and we would have made some today.

Plenty of people use wine for fruitcake. If you've got a big fruitcake, soak it in wine, and that fruitcake will last from one Christmas to the next. It'll last a year. Get enough wine in it, ain't much fruitcake then. It's about like drinking wine.

Any sweet grape or just any grape that's got a sugar content [will make wine]. I've made blackberry and grape. Nothing but grape, blackberry, and wild cherry. Wild cherries make good wine. You make cherry wine just like you make your blackberry wine, except it'll have a cherry flavor. Them wild cherries have got a lot of flavor.

You gotta use either a glass or plastic container to put the berries in. Or you need a churn—it's the best. Just an old clay churn seems to do. You can take a gallon of berries and you can use a gallon glass, say, a pickle jar or a milk jar, and that will work real good for 1 gallon of wine.

You want to let the berries get good and ripe. Then you got to mash 'em up—grind 'em up somehow to burst them. You could use a vegetable colander and grind 'em up, or take your hand and squeeze 'em up, or put them in a bucket or container and mash them, just so you get them squished up, mashed up. You gotta bust them. That way the juice will come out of

Carlton English

them. If you don't, it won't.

Blackberries or grapes, neither one has very much juice. You would take a half-a-pound of sugar and put it with a quart of warm water and let it dissolve and pour it into your berries and stir it. That will make a liquid, you see. That's where you get your amount of wine. Either one of them, like the grape, you want them to get good and ripe and you want to mash those up. You want to burst them. They won't ferment until they're bursted.

You would get about a half-a-gallon [of wine from a gallon of blackberries]. The berries wouldn't have no more than 2 teacups of juice. Where you would get your wine would be that sugar and the water you added. You use [the water and sugar] for a body or a filler and that is what makes it work.

And on the grapes, I'd pick about 5 gallons of grapes and put 'em in a 10-gallon wooden barrel, and I'd work those about thirty days. In 5 gallons of grapes, I'd put 5 pounds of sugar and a gallon of water.

Go to somewhere like Winn-Dixie and get that powdered yeast. To a gallon of wine, you use one of those packs, which will be about a spoonful of yeast. It'll make it work off better. You could put corn in it if you had sprouty corn, what they call malt. You sprout your corn and crush it up, and put it in there. That acts the same thing as yeast. It's real good to use corn, sprouted corn, to make malt [syrup]. Use about a teacupful of corn per gallon of wine. That'll make it work. It won't change [the taste] much, just make it work a little better. Put a little yeast and that will sure start it to fermentin' and making wine and taste better.

But you don't want your wine more than about 2 or 3 inches to the top [of the container], since when it works it'll foam up real heavy.

Put a cloth over it or a lid, but you don't want it airtight. It will burst a glass jar if you cap it too tight. It'll work and that air has got to come out of there. You want to cover [the mix] good so that what you call the sour gnats won't get in there. Yeah, you want to keep those sour gnats out of it. They'll get in it and that there will make vinegar. And vinegar will kill that wine. You sure gotta keep it covered so those gnats won't get in it. They'll just swarm after it. Like if there's a banana or apple or grapes layin' out there and just in a few hours, they'll be covered with those sour gnats. I don't know where they come from, but [they get in there and] that stops the bacteria and makes vinegar. You get vinegar in that wine and it will all turn to vinegar—it won't make wine.

[After you cover it,] just put it in a cool place out of the sun. Don't put it in the sun. Just put it in the shade, in the building, in the back room, or in the smokehouse, somewhere where it's cool. Always keep it at just a cool, normal temperature.

And you leave it for about—well, blackberries take about five or six days and grapes will take ten or twelve days. You let that work off good. You can tell when it has quit fermenting. It will settle. You go back and resugar that and add a little more water. [Enough to fill your container back up.] And it will go right back to working—go right back to work.

You want to do that two more times. To a gallon of berries, each time you work it, it will gain 5 percent alcohol, see. You want to work it off to where it will be about 18 or 20 percent. That is about as strong as you can get it. It will take twenty days to complete making it. And then you strain it off through a strainer or a cloth or something and that will get all that pummy off there, and you won't have nothing but the liquid. And you just take that and put it in a glass container or jars. Cap it up, but don't cap it tight for it will [continue to] ferment a little bit along maybe six or twelve days, according to the temperature.

I've had it where it didn't work. It would turn to vinegar or just wouldn't do. If you don't get it just right, just the right amount of berries, right amount of sugar, right amount of water, it won't work, but yeast will sure make it works. You get your alcohol from your sugar, but the yeast will completely work it on out. It'll make it ferment on out better and quicker.

"When we come back, it was all busted to pieces."

~NELSON CABE~

Just pick yer grapes off and mash 'em up. Take yer hands and bust every grape, you know, mash until you've got every one busted. Put you about 5 gallons or 4 gallons or whatever yer jar'll hold. I make it in churns. You can't make it in a metal container—have to have wood or porcelain. I put about 5 pounds of sugar to about 5 gallons of grapes when I first put it in to work off. Some people adds a little bit of water, but I never did add no water to mine. Somebody said that you could use a little bit of yeast because that would make it start working a little quicker, but I never did use any. Might be better if you'd use a little bit. I guess you might wind up with about 2.5 or 3 gallons out of a 5-gallon jar.

I use a churn dash on mine [to cover the wine]. [It is] an old-timey wooden lid that goes down on it. Put you a cloth under it and put you a dash down on it. Then slit a hole [in the cloth]. Then put you a hose pipe in [the hole] and pour paraffin wax around it and on top of it and that seals the hole up. Then you stick the other end of the hose pipe down in a quart can of water. While the wine works that quart can of water will bubble. It's better if you work it off with a hose pipe so it can't get no air. Let it work till that water quits bubbling. Then you take the cover off and strain it. Then put it back in your churn and put sugar in it again. Then let it work again 'bout seven days. You watch it. You can tell when it quits working. It'll bubble a little bit along. Then, when it quits that, why, you just take it off and strain all your juice out and just do away with your grapes, put your juice back in a churn, and add you some more sugar. I work mine off about four times. You don't want to add too much sugar. Don't put as much in it the rest of the time as you do the first time. You can kindly taste it along and tell if it's sweet enough.

I strain mine with white cloth. Some people take [womens'] stocking hoses—strain with that. Most people, when they make wine, they keep straining it off until it foams a little bit. We've made wine from white grapes and it makes good grape wine. It makes you sick if it gets too sweet.

I had some blowed up last I made. We put it down there in the basement. We was gonna leave and wanted to strain it and put it in cans before we left. We strained it and fixed it and put it in cans. I put some of it in old whiskey bottles I got and some in regular wine bottles. When we come back it was all busted to pieces. [Laughs.] Happened we'd left it on the sink and it all went down the sink. If we hadn't, it woulda been a mess. It would've been all right if I hadn't sealed it real tight.

We didn't make much wine last year or the year before last. I never use it for anything much but fruitcake. I always had to buy it, and it is pretty expensive to buy it.

In making my juice I put 2 cups of grapes and a cup of sugar in a half-a-gallon jar and pour hot water over it, then put it in a hot-water bath and seal it up and cook it for twenty minutes. It won't be juice then—it takes it a while to turn to juice and be real good juice.

If I make jelly, I mash my grapes up and put just a little water and start them to cooking and cook them till they are done and strain the juice off them. [Add sugar.] Now, you cook the grapes and sugar and you set it up. It'll still be clear enough nearly when you set it up.

My daddy used to make homebrew, but I don't know how he made it—I wasn't old enough to know how he did it. I have a brother that messes with it now—once in a while he'll make brandy and stuff like that, but I don't know how he makes it. He makes peach brandy. I don't know if he makes homebrew now or not. I never heard him say anything about homebrew, but I do know he makes brandy. I don't know of anybody that makes homebrew. Everybody we have talked to so far say it's cheaper to buy beer out of the store than to try to make a living. It costs so much to make it, all you lose is the fun of it.

"It has just a delightful flavor."

~LUCY KIMBELL~

Wine can be made out of any kind of fruit. You can even make wine out of tomatoes. (Tomato is sort of a mixture between a vegetable and a fruit.) Anything that has natural sugar in it, you can make wine out of. Most people around here use grapes because they're plentiful. Blackberries, plums—don't hear plums much—but I made some plum last year and it was some of the best wine I've ever made. I 'specially like peaches and white grapes. Most people make peach brandy, but you can make wine out of peaches, too, or rhubarb. Just anything that has natural sugar in it. I've made blackberry, Concord, rhubarb, white grape, red grape, and black grape wines. The white grape is smoother. It has just a delightful flavor—I don't know how to describe it to you—much better than the red grapes.

[The materials I use to make wine include] a big vat that I start my fruit off in. That's to let it ferment in. Then I have the big 5-gallon containers that have the screw top with the little thing that the air goes through [air lock]. You can tell that I'm not really a [professional] winemaker—I just know how to do it and what I use to do it. Then you have to have a siphon. I have a hydrometer because I do watch my sugar content. That way you can tell how much alcohol content you have. And I use Campden™ tablets to keep down the bacteria.

I start off with 5 gallons of fruit, [crush it up]. I use a big spoon with holes in it, and I just crush it along the sides of the container. That helps

Richard Edwards helps Lucy Kimbell measure sugar

loosen it up. Then I put 4 Campden™ tablets in it. I use Campden™ tablets because if the wrong kind of bacteria gets in there, it will turn to vinegar, and you'll lose quite an investment. Suppose you go out and buy forty dollars' worth of blackberries, you put ten dollars' worth of sugar in there or more, [and it turns to vinegar]. You've lost quite a bit of money. So I don't risk that. I use the Campden™. My neighbor up here made some of the prettiest wine. It smelled so good—and I tasted it. Well, she didn't use the Campden™ tablets in it, and it turned out to be vinegar. So she lost all that. She hasn't had the courage to try again.

To that amount [of fruit] the sugar will get up to about 1.12 percent, and that is pretty close to 22 percent alcohol. I can't really tell you the exact amount of sugar. I can say that it would probably take about 5 pounds of sugar to 5 gallons [of fruit]. This would yield about 3 gallons of wine. If the fruit is really ripe, and it should be, it doesn't take as much sugar. I use regular wine yeast that I order. I think you can use regular yeast, but I wouldn't know how much to use. I put one package of wine yeast in that 5 gallons. I don't know what the difference is in what I have and what you buy in the store.

I let the ingredients sit for five to seven days. You always keep that covered to keep the varmints out—the gnats and things like that it draws. But don't cover it with plastic or anything, because it needs to breathe, so I cover it with that big huck towel that the air can get through. It's kind of a thick towel—a bird's eye. It's just something I had that works. (I didn't go out and buy a lot of stuff, just the corker and hydrometer.) I go back every day to stir it. It takes longer for it to ferment [if the weather is cool]. The ideal temperature is around 70 degrees [F]. Sometimes it gets hotter than that, but at night it cools off, so it sorta offsets it.

After about seven days of fermentation, I strain it. I have a big colander and I let it go through that first. I don't force it through because I don't want all that pulp and stuff in there. Then I take the juice I get and just let it run through cheesecloth. That way I get a pretty clear juice and I'm ready to start my working time. That's when I put my Campden™ tablets in again. When I'm through with the fermentation and I'm ready to stop it, or I just want to clear up the wine, I put in the Campden™. You put in your [Campden™ tablets], stop your fermentation, and then you let it set. Campden™ is actually poison if you sit down and eat it, but in using it in minute amounts, it keeps

Lucy Kimbell

the very harmful bacteria out.

Next, start racking it all, depending on how quickly it sets up. That's when you siphon it off and leave your dregs in the bottom. Then you siphon it off again, later, when it has set again. But you don't want to keep fermenting, so you have to stop your fermentation and then you continue racking. The very last thing I put in it, maybe the last two or three times I'm going to rack, I put this stuff called Sparkolloid™ in it, and that makes the sediment go to the bottom and it clears it up and makes it really pretty and clear. And, then, the bottles. I use cork tops because I don't have a capper to seal off the air, so I don't use that method. I use the corks and I've got a corker. I beg my wine bottles from people who buy wine, or I get bottles that fit my special cork top.

Fall is a good time to make wine. Of course, you do it when the fruit is ready—it doesn't really matter the time of year. For this area, the grapes are better in the fall. In mid- or early-summer, you get plums and other fruits: peaches, blackberries, and things. From there on out, whenever fruit becomes available. You could make wine up to November.

I just make wine to enjoy it. I give mine away. I make it and give it away for gifts and things. We don't drink that much of it. I put it in my fruitcakes, but usually, if the subject comes up, and if I've got a bottle, I'll open it.

"It's something nice to have on hand."

~SCOTT BROOKS~

I've been making wine on and off for about five years. It's just something you know—like making jelly.

The easiest process I've found to make grape wine is called the "balloon process." I learned it from Bonnie Handte over in Ellijay [Georgia]. Pour two 12-ounce cans of Welch's grape juice into a gallon jug. Add 4 cups of sugar and a ¼ teaspoon of winemaking yeast to your jug. Put a balloon over the mouth of the jug, shake it up, and then let the juice ferment for two weeks. The balloon acts as your fermentation lock. The balloon blows up and doesn't allow air to come in.

Today, I'm mixing blackberries and elderberries together. It's going to be a combination of the two. It's going to have the tendency to taste more like grape wine, but I'm hoping there'll be a blackberry taste to it, too.

I heard about somebody that did this. They mixed rhubarb with blueberries. Rhubarb has a high acid content to it and so you can use that to balance your blueberries out—make your blueberries have more acid.

I picked at least a gallon of elderberries today. What I'll do is just mash them up and get the juice out. Then I'll measure the juice into a bowl and pour it into a 5-gallon jug. I also picked a full gallon of blackberries. They are a domestic-type blackberry, not the ones we usually find out in a field. I'll just go ahead and crush them up, get all the juice out of them. Some people strain the blackberry juice real good to get some of the pulp out. I may get a little pulp or seed in there, but that doesn't matter because it's all good. It helps to make the taste of the blackberries come out when it's fermenting in the jug.

When you go to picking your blackberries or elderberries, you can pick some that are real ripe and some that are not ripe. You need the acid in the greener berries, so that the acid and the sugar will make a gas. That forms the alcohol.

I put in 2 liters of blackberry juice and 2 liters of elderberry juice. That will make a little over a gallon. For now, I'll put 4 pounds of sugar in the jug. Later, I may add more. I'm also going to put in a full quart of honey. My wine comes out a little bit stronger than commercial wine, probably because a lot of times we add more sugar to it than the commercial makers do. And store-bought wine may be watered down.

I'll add a quart of warm water to the juice to help dissolve the sugar. I will also add two winemaking Campden™ tablets per gallon to start the fermentation. I'll then add water to make the entire volume about 4½ gallons into this 5-gallon jug because it needs space at the top of the jug to expand.

I remember using city water at one time, but city water tends to kill the yeast because it has chlorine in it. Now, even though well water has been processed enough to get the germs out, you get a little bit of the kill in it also. For me, it'd be kind of difficult to climb all the way up that hill to bring back good, clear, unprocessed water. I've used Crystal Springs™ bottled water before. It doesn't have any chlorine in it. It's just pure water. That's the only bottled water I've ever used. I usually make wine by the gallon out of that bottled water, and it works real well.

I have used yeast before, but I just don't have any right now. I would usually buy a winemaking yeast to put in, but I've found that using raw honey will produce the yeast that we need to make the juice ferment. The reason I'm trying honey is to figure out the cheapest way to make wine because it is difficult to get the yeast. I have to go to Atlanta to pick it up.

You can tell how high the alcohol content is just by measuring with a hydrometer. You need to measure it with the hydrometer before you put the fermentation lock on and after you take it off, when you go to tap it off, or what we call "racking." I've measured this batch two times and it usually runs about 15 percent, which is around 7 percent more than commercial wines.

The whole process for fermentation takes about two weeks, depending on the weather and the atmosphere. The slower the processing is, the better the wine is. Sometimes it'll come out and be bubbly, almost like champagne. You can cut [the bubbling] down by putting gelatin finings in it. You can buy straight gelatin in the store and let it soak for an hour. Then boil it for fifteen or twenty minutes and pour it into the wine. This causes the sediment to go to the bottom. You can add ascorbic acid to keep the process of bubbling from rebubbling again. Ascorbic acid is like a preservative—therefore, preventing renewed fermentation. You can get the ascorbic acid at a wine art store. If the wine is not sweet enough, you can add more sugar just before pouring it into the wine bottles.

[When I'm ready to bottle the wine,] I put a little oil on the bottom of the corks. I like to use olive oil. It has a tendency to slide a lot better than peanut oil. Then I slide the corks into the bottles. Push the corks straight in. This is where it gets touchy, but just be patient and try to be consistent. Those corks will stop up your wine bottles just like you see in wine stores. To avoid problems with corking, it would be wise to invest in a twenty-dollar corker.

You can pick up extra wine bottles from neighbors and friends who drink the regular, store-bought wine. Just remember to sterilize whatever you put your wine in. Also, wash your bottles out with baking soda using a bottle brush. It gets down in the bottom to get the sediment out. The soda will usually sweeten the bottle.

I never strain the wine into the bottles because usually I'll let it set with the gelatin finings to let the particles drop down to the bottom. I siphon off the wine, leaving the sediment in the bottom. If you're careful, you can draw the wine up with a minimum of pulp or sediment in it.

It's really best to store the bottles of wine in a room that stays about 65 to 75 degrees [F]. Some people put them in an old refrigerator if they have one. It's still best to do it the old-fashioned way—have the bottles on a tilt, where the wine leans down and is absorbed into the cork. That makes a real good seal. And with any homemade wine, there'll be a certain amount of sediment no matter how you pour it off, so let the bottles set for at least two weeks. Let the sediment settle to the bottom.

It seems that berry wines tend to—well, several people have said "Your wine gives me a headache the next morning." Now, it's not because they

Scott Brooks

drink a lot. It's because there is something in it that causes you to have a headache. There may be too much sugar in it.

The products for making wine are still quite expensive. The main thing I'm trying to do is to avoid a lot of expense. I estimate it's not more than seven or eight dollars for me to make 5 gallons. Now, this wine cost me a little bit extra because I had to buy the honey. The cost may double when you're starting out because of the equipment you'll need.

Most of the wine I've made this year is already drunk up. Once you get to making it, it seems that you're either giving it to friends or drinking it all at get-togethers. The best way to avoid running out is to keep making your batches every two weeks. Keep processing so you'll have a supply by the end of the year. I gave eight bottles of the stuff away last year for Christmas. It's like a stocking stuffer.

You can develop a taste for homemade wine because it is much stronger. It's different from any of your Burgundy or other commercial grape wines. It comes out stronger. It's not watered down quite as much.

It's really unique, the way wine is made. It takes time and it's hard to do but, really, there's a sort of novelty to it. It's something nice to have on hand when your friends come over.

"Wine is the most wholesome beverage in the world. That goes back to the Bible."

~ARLYN & BILL PARK~

BILL: We make grape juice mostly from the Concord grapes and some from the blackberry. We have several jars of juice. We enjoy grape juice. I make blackberry [wine] more or less as a family tradition. Our family always made blackberry wine when I was growing up. They used it for medical purposes. We keep it in case we have a' upset stomach. We take a little blackberry wine. My wife uses it for cooking and marinating meat [after] the wines go to vinegar.

We always let our children know what wine was like. My parents raised me up the same way. That's why I became interested in making wine—because I helped them as long as I can remember.

ARLYN: I think you can overuse anything, but they were always allowed a little taste. I had a niece and nephew just here this weekend, and they wanted to taste their mama's wine. They were allowed to taste it, but just one little sip.

BILL: Neither of our two children drink anything heavy. They've never even had a highball. We would let them taste it so they would know what we were drinking, particularly with the wine because we make several varieties. One year, when I was much younger I made, I think, twelve different varieties. And I decided after that year I would devote most of my winemaking to the grapes.

ARLYN: We give a lot of wine as gifts. We go to parties and dinners and take a bottle of wine with us. That's where some of the wine goes. We're not heavy wine drinkers. We like to have a glass of wine before dinner and maybe with dinner, but not just to sit down and drink one glass after the other.

BILL: People say you can make a gallon for your own use. Of course, I don't think the law would come looking for you if you make a gallon. Someone would report you if you were making a gallon of brandy over there in that house. They would have to send the sheriff to come get you. No sheriff is going to look for you if you're making a gallon [of wine]. You have to have a license if you make 200 gallons, but I don't know of any family that can use 200 gallons. They would be floating or something. I make 15 or 20 gallons—some years a little more and some years a little less.

Wine is the most wholesome beverage in the world. That goes back to the Bible. The Lord gave Paul grapes and told him to make wine.

There's a difference in the white and the red wine. The red wine is fermented with the pulp. That's where you get your color. All the color is in the hull. For white wine you crush your grapes and strain the juice out immediately, before you ferment. You get no pectin in your juice. You add your yeast and your sugar the same way you do the other, only you're just working with juice. The different grapes make a different flavor. Some make it darker: The darker the color and the riper the grapes, the better the wine.

The white wine has a less, I guess you would say, astringent taste. That would be sort of a vinegarish taste. I would say wine on the road to being vinegar. That's why you use the air lock to keep the wild yeast from getting back into your jug while it's working off.

We'd like to get hold of some nice, white grapes that would make wine. We have those grapes [muscadines] growing over the persimmon tree. We got 4½ bushels last year off of our grapes. We don't have any white ones and we'd like to this fall.

Grapes or fruit, I put 'em into the crusher first, and if I'm goin' to make red wine, I'll leave the pulp with the juice. I also use sugar and water. These are the three basic things I use to make wine. I use the yeast, but the fruit has a wild yeast that makes it ferment on its own. I add yeast and ferment it so many days.

To make my wine, I use Concord, wild muscadines, and fox grapes. I

Bill Park

have this Concord grape that we call the Mid-South grape and a French-type grape that was sent to the extension people here several years ago to experiment with—to see how it would grow in this area. Wilbur Maney turned 'em over to Bob Massey to raise and to experiment with them.

Two years ago I went to Wilbur Maney to find out about getting these grapes and he says go and talk to Bob Massey because he had some and turned 'em over to Bob to see what they were like. Bob Massey sent me out to look at 'em. They were beautiful—about as big as the end of my little finger. Solid black. So after talking to Bob Massey a while and explaining to him that I wanted to make wine with them and to experiment with them, he turned the grapes over to me to experiment with. The experiment the first year came out real good. Last year we experimented again, and that's when I made several different types of the wine from 'em. They make a real good wine. I'm going to plant some of these grapes on my own. I've got about fifty plants to plant now, mostly this French-type grape and the Concord and the muscadine. [They say] the Concord don't make a good wine, but I differ with them. I think I've proven a pretty good wine with the Concord grapes. I think the quality of your wine is in the way you work it off.

Go through your grapes and pick out the bad ones and the leaves. You remove the bad ones along with the green ones too—because it doesn't help the wine. (Normally, I get 'em picked a little cleaner than this, but I did this hurriedly.) The rule of thumb is: It takes a gallon of grapes to produce a gallon of wine. Some grapes have more natural sugar than others, and that's why French-type makes good wine. It's no good for eating.

Let's say to make 5 gallons of red wine, we have gathered a bushel of grapes. When we pick these grapes from the stems, they'll fill a 5-gallon bucket. We wash 'em and then mash 'em, crush 'em. Then put 'em in the plastic bucket to ferment. I do add yeast—wine yeast. It's developed in Germany and it's especially for making wine. By adding the yeast it only takes three days and three nights to ferment. If you don't use yeast, it takes ten days and ten nights to ferment.

The Campden™ tablet can be used for a dozen different purposes. It can be used to start your fermentation and it can be used to stop your fermentation. If you work your wine right, you don't need it. I find that my wine tastes better without any chemicals added whatsoever. You never use soap with your wine utensils or bottles. The only way you can sterilize them is with chemicals like the Campden™ tablets. They're made out of a chemical you can buy at a drugstore. If you want to stop the fermentation of your wine, you mix one tablet to each gallon of wine. I don't want to stop fermentating—I want it to work itself off.

I ferment my wine in 5-gallon plastic buckets or stainless-steel churns. Cover 'em with cheesecloth to keep the bugs out. Around a 70-degree [F] temp is the ideal temperature for wine to work off. Always keep [the wine] in the dark. Never let real bright sunlight get to it. (The only thing the light does to it is bleach it. It doesn't affect the taste of the wine.) [I let the wine age] six to eight months before anybody can taste it—at least six to eight months. Most of mine goes about a year. I haven't made any wine at this time of the year, but these grapes and fruit all came to me and I was forced into it.

To separate the pulp from the juice, you [use] a grape press. You put your fermented pulp into the press. The inside of it is perforated so that the juice squeezes out between it and the outer ring. And the bottom is also perforated so the juice can go through the bottom. This bottom fits inside of the inside ring. Then you just turn the crank down and it forces the juice out. By using this, instead of squeezing the juice out by hand, you gain, out of a bushel of grapes, about an extra gallon of juice. Just tighten it down. Each time you give it a half a turn, some more juice'll come out. When I hold it at that point, it gets harder to squeeze. You keep squeezing until the juice gets almost pink. There's another way you can do it: You can do it with a sieve—let it drain out. Or you can drain it through a cloth and squeeze it out. That's a lot of extra work. We used to do it that way.

I use between 2½ and 3 pounds of sugar. Use no substitutes whatsoever. You *can* ferment the wine without sugar or yeast. If you gather ripe grapes and mash 'em up, they'll ferment on their own and they'll work off on their own and turn into wine. This would be a dry [wine]. To some people it wouldn't taste good.

Be sure that you have a full gallon-and-a-half of juice. Then add the sugar. Pour the juice into a 5-gallon jug. Then I add 15 pounds of sugar. To add the sugar, you dissolve it [in water] to make a simple syrup, then add it. It mixes in faster and makes work. Then you let it work a couple of days and you start adding the rest of the sugar. You mix maybe a pound at a time in the syrup form. You mix 5 pounds of sugar into a simple syrup and add a pint to a quart of water each day. Use lukewarm water, never hot. That would kill your yeast. Do that over a period of ten days. Then each day after that you add a pint or a quart of water until you get your jug filled up.

When your wine is working off, what it's actually doin' is—well, you've got sugar and yeast fighting each other. Them fighting each other is what makes alcohol. When they've exhausted each other, your wine ceases to work and you have a finished wine with a certain percentage of alcohol. In wine, you measure alcohol by proof. In whiskey, you measure alcohol by volume. A wine that has an alcohol of 24 proof is equal to 12 percent by volume, if you measure it by volume. If you drank a water glass of wine, you would get just as drunk as if you drank a highball made with 2 or 3 ounces of whiskey. If you try to make your alcohol proof too high, you have an oversweet wine. [Adding sugar is] the only way you can get it. The highest proof you can possibly get, in homemade wine, is 36 proof [18 percent]. The only way you can get it higher is to fortify it. And then you ruin it. I like it on the dry [side]. My wife likes it on the medium-dry. Most of our friends like it on the sweet side. But too-sweet wine is not good. A lot of people make wine and put a lot of sugar in it. Alcohol is immaterial to me as far as my wine. I'm making it for the quality of the flavor, the bouquet (which is how it smells), and the cleanness—how clean it comes out.

You use a hydrometer after you crush your fruit. You put a test tube near full (about two inches from the top). You take a reading with your hydrometer to see how much sugar content your grapes have. You start sweetenin' your grapes after you separate the pulp from the juice. Add enough sugar to give you a reading of 22, which is the average reading to get to make good, sweet wine. Then do your test tube and take a reading. Then, after your wine has completely worked out, you put some of your wine in the test tube again and take a reading. The reading you get then, you subtract from your original reading and that gives you your percentage of alcohol. You subtract your 10 from 22. You would have approximately a percentage of 12 percent alcohol. Then you siphon it off the bottle that it worked off in and put it in a new bottle and let it age. The reason you siphon it off is because the sediment that comes while it's working off would make a taste in your wine.

The air lock don't form a vacuum. It locks out the outside air, which contains wild yeast. Basically, you're locking out the wild yeast. If you let it ferment without an air lock on it, put a piece of cheesecloth over it to keep the bugs out. When you're making wine, if you don't have an air lock on tight, you have a lot of wineflies accumulate. You see some people have so many wineflies they can't find the wine.

With the old-fashioned way—this is why it's been improved—you never knew whether your wine was going to vinegar or not when you didn't cover it or do something with it. That's when they started making the little tube going from the glass jar to the bottle of water [air lock].

"If it'll knock you on your back, it's robust!"

~R. C. DOBBINS~

I used to make many kinds of wine. Now, I stick to fox grape and muscadine. Every once in a while, I'll make something different when the stores have a special wine-red peach, or a particularly red plum of California. On occasion, I'll make white wine if I have the grapes, and I do have some of my own grapes this year. But I don't prefer white wine. To me, white wine just doesn't have the character a red wine has. And I know a red wine will give you a headache quicker than a white wine.

The English make wine out of just about everything—even beets! I come from people that used to make tomato butter, which was a sweet jam. It had a good flavor. It wouldn't touch strawberries, as far as I was concerned, but it was all right.

I read quite a bit about wine and winemaking, and I've been influenced by the opinions of some professionals that say, "This grape is no good and that grape is no good." They don't use strong expressions like that. They say, "Very interesting," which incidentally brings up a point: When they discuss wine, and you hear "robust flavor" and "strong" and "bouquet" and so forth, it seems that the only real terms you can discuss are the bouquet of the wine and whether it's too dry or sweet. And I've gotten to the point where I like a semi-dry wine, so I make it like that. People either like it or they don't. My son in New York prefers a dry wine and he keeps picking on me, saying I should make a drier wine. It's very easy to make a dry wine.

Most fermentations will ferment out until the wine is very dry. And then, just add sugar.

But I find that muscadine and fox grape give such a good color and strong bouquet, and they ferment easily. Blueberries don't ferment easily. I don't like blueberry wine. Elderberry wine is a problem for most people—it has a little aftertaste. If you've ever eaten cherries or blackberries, and chewed the little stem, it's bitter—and you sort of get an aftertaste like that. I kind of like elderberry wine, but most people don't.

When most people say "strong" wine, they are referring to the alcohol content. The commercial people call it "robust." If it'll knock you on your back, it's robust! But even strong wine, as I mentioned before, can only get up to about 13 percent or 14 percent unless they fortify it—they do that with some of the wines. But the amateur can only get 13 percent to 14 percent—I guess you could make it over 14 percent. To get the proof, you double your percentage. So that would bring it up to 26 to 28 proof.

I usually make my wine in the fall, late September, because that's when I get my muscadine grapes and fox grapes. Suppose someone just drove in now and said, "Hey, I've got some early muscadine grapes." I'm not ready to start making wine. I've got you people sitting here. It's too warm. I want to go swimming. I just don't want to start. I would just put those grapes in the freezer. It doesn't hurt them. In fact, they would probably crush out easier once they're frozen. And so many times I just put them in a plastic bag and dump them in the freezer until I'm ready. Nobody likes to make wine if they don't feel like it.

The materials I use to make wine are either a large aluminum container or a plastic container, plastic tubs, and plastic barrels. You ought to make an amount you can handle easily for your equipment and storage space. Five-gallon batches work out fine with me, even though I sometimes make six or eight 5-gallon batches at the same time. I use those kinds of containers, especially if it's a recipe I can work with easily, that I've done so many times. After you run it through the primary stage where you have the sugar and the pulp and the water and yeast and everything working together, after eight or ten days, you then siphon it off into the secondary stage, and that's usually another 5-gallon jug and you put a breather cap on there with water in it. That allows the carbon dioxide to pass off without taking away any other fresh air.

There are a number of ingredients I use—all of which you don't *have* to use. I use, of course, the fruit and sugar and yeast. Sometimes I add acid. I do have a test for acid, but I don't think it's real accurate. I go with my rule of thumb in adding yeast and I use an acid that is a blend [of several different acids], which seems to work out for grape wine. It adds tartness to the wine. Also, if I'm making wine with a grape that seems to be a bland grape to my taste, I add just a touch of tannin—this gives it a little character. So, you don't *need* the acid or tannin. You might make an excellent wine without them. And another thing, if you add pectin enzyme, it will help you get a more complete fermentation. You get more color out of the skins and really more wine flavoring in the pulp. But here again, if you just add yeast to crushed grapes and sugar and water, you might make a good-tasting wine. I think the more you work at it, the more you try to refine it to eliminate these times when you say, "Oh geez, that did not work out well."

I also use a wine clarifier called Speedy Bentinite™. It's for the wine to clear, settle out so it looks like wine as you know it. If it doesn't, you can take some of the wine out, put it into a bottle, about half full, take a couple of teaspoons of this [Bentinite™] and put it in there. This acts like mud, turns it into a glop. But if you keep shaking it, so it doesn't have a chance to do that, you get this milky solution in here and then pour that into the top of the wine. If it's in one of those 5-gallon glass containers, I just wriggle it around so it sprays all around the top. Now, you've made the whole batch of wine cloudy—then it settles out just as though you had poured something in it. It's just so damn heavy.

It just goes right on down through, and it takes all these little particles out of it that are debris of some kind or another. Lately, I have not had to use that. I think the wine loses a little character when you do that. But plum wine, particularly, doesn't seem to settle out easily and quickly, and I've used Bentinite™ and it'll come out just as clean. The last plum wine I made was quite white. It looked like it had been made from a white grape. It just had no color in it at all. I attribute that partly to the sun because all the plums I've used have been pink- or reddish-skinned. You should get a slight color. I use Campden™ tablets. Let me get one and read you that chemical formula— sodium metabisulfide. Of course, you all remember your chemistry. Sulfide is different than sulfate. You put in about one tablet per gallon. (They're about as big as aspirin.)

R. C. Dobbins

The fumes pass off in twenty-four hours, so you're leaving the wine must. ("Must" is what you call the batch before it turns to wine.) I usually put everything in but the yeast, put in the Campden™ tablets, and forty-eight hours later I put in the yeast.

The yeast will usually give you instructions on how to [proportion the ingredients]. That's not critical. The temperature is critical in that it should be around 60 to 65 degrees [F] while it's fermenting. Sometimes it doesn't matter if it gets a little warmer. If it gets cooler than that it may stop—and you get what you call a stuck fermentation. And sometimes it's very difficult to get started again.

If it's stuck and stays stuck you just have nothing. You have a sweet syrupy concoction, then the yeast will have died out in it and you need something to start it out again. I usually start a new batch with separate juice and get it fermenting and dump that into the one that stopped. Be sure the temperature is correct. The ingredients, I guess, are not critical if you're making enough wine.

I once made a batch of pear wine, about 3 gallons, and that turned to vinegar—3 gallons of vinegar is a lot. I tell you, we had great vinegar and oil for salads for a while.

I go by the rule of thumb on the sugar, but I double-check it for specific gravity. Right around 1.01 seems to make the strongest wine that I can make and still have a good fermentation. [I check the specific gravity] after I've mixed the sugar in and before I add the yeast. [This would be after the pulp is crushed and you've added whatever water you're going to add.] Then, you have a little hydrometer and you fill it up, and the little measuring device will float up and you read at that level where it's floating and it'll tell you what the specific gravity is. There is also another reading on there. It's called Brix and it's a similar reading, and it's used in winemaking. About 25 Brix will make you the strongest wine possible. If you take a wine that is percentage-wise around 5 or 6 or 7, maybe even 8 or 9 percent, the wine will not store. It just gets very bland and loses its character completely. And the same with acid. I made some wine here about eight years ago that I thought was very good, and I gave a bottle to my daughter, who kept it about six years. I was talking about it one day, and she said she'd send me a bottle back. Well, she sent it back and we were pleased to get it. We thought it would be so good and it was *terrible*. It was just as flat as flavored water. Exactly. This was partly because it didn't have enough alcohol in it and partly because it didn't have enough acid. This was one thing the old-timers missed was the acid. However, the wine will taste good up to a year, a year and a half. That's why it's hard for an amateur to make a "vintage" wine, which is a wine known by its particular year.

Are you familiar with the way the French make classic champagne? The classic French way of making champagne is to start with their best wines and, if they are satisfied with the quality, they put a temporary cork in the bottle. Then they put that bottle in a place where it will ferment because they add a new fermentation wine or additional yeast. Then they put that bottle in a position where it is vertical, but upside down. And a man comes by. He will twist the bottle periodically and give it a shake to keep the residue of the dead yeast and other debris down in the cork. And when that has finished fermenting [the second time], it is now truly champagne. They then freeze the neck of the bottle and then this man with the French name comes by and removes the temporary cork because it is an icicle at that point. He then puts his thumb over the bottle until he can add the new cork. Generally, they don't lose enough of the wine that they have to add any new wine, but if they do, they will add enough to bring it up to the exact spot. They put on this fresh champagne cork shaped like a mushroom, and they put a metal bridle over it and twist that bridle until it holds that cork tightly in there. There's a glass rim on the bottle so it's locked in there. They then put on their special foil and label and so forth. Now that's the classic method. They do make it like Americans under the pressure system now, but the truly classic vintage champagnes—the ones with the big reputations—do it the old-fashioned way.

I make champagne the way this English amateur told me to do it. After you have wine that you think is okay, you add more yeast. I had to guess at that—you don't have to add much. And I added a level teaspoon of sugar. I shook it up and put a temporary cork in it. Temporary because I didn't know if the bottle would blow up or what it would do. At the end of about six weeks, I took the cork off and it popped. It was under pressure and it was not good, but I thought, "Well, that's really going to work." So when I made six or eight bottles of it, I put the wine corks on and I opened three in a row and they were just flat. Just plain, ordinary wine. One day my wife said, "We're going to have something special, why don't you break out one of those special bottles of wine and make it a good one for a change." So I brought one up, and I was talking to her and not paying any attention and, when I took that bridle off, that cork went "Pow!" It was really good champagne. We drank the whole bottle standing right there because it foamed so much. And I'm convinced that the next batch had a little better look. I used about ¾ of a teaspoon of sugar.

[Mr. Dobbins picks up a bottle of his wine.] When somebody comes in and picks up a bottle of your wine and says, "Hurray for you!" and shakes it, you're going to learn to hate them because whatever debris is in there [is going to make the wine cloudy again]. Even in commercial wine there is some debris.

Can you see that stuff floating around in there? Now, to get that out, I'll have to siphon it off. Look what happens if I just tip it. [He pours some in a glass.] See, it gets all cloudy and there'll be little things floating around like bugs or whatever or dead yeast and so forth. And you don't even really have to shake it that much, if you just pour it. Of course, commercial champagnes, they could afford to spend a little more time with it because it's expensive and you pay for a good, clean wine and so forth. But the true wine would have no [incomplete] fermentation and little debris. They're like pies or cakes. You can have a good pie or cake and you just don't care for it, like maybe you don't care for raspberry pie or raspberry cake or whatever. And the same with wines. There could be an excellent wine or a peach-type wine and you just don't care for it. But there is a wine similar that you'll like, so don't give up!

Someone told me that the South is starting to put in wineries. He said they have muscadine wines commercially made, and he said it looks like the South may try to catch up with the northern states on winemaking. He mentioned one just outside of Atlanta that he knew of. They had their own vineyards and ran the business. There is a winery real close to here. I don't know where exactly, but I know there's one.

There are tricks to making wine. If you want a good fermentation to really start off right, bubbling and foaming, you can start it off with about a pint of orange juice. Take a pint of orange juice, which is not really a strong-flavored thing, and dilute it till you have maybe almost a quart of orange juice and water and sugar and put your yeast in that.

Now you have it in a quart jar. I usually put [the fermenting wine] up on the mantel right where I can watch it in the house and, sometimes, if I'm having friends over and they don't know anything about making wine, I even put a bubbler up there—about 5 gallons of wine just so they can see what's going on. Anyway, this orange juice, you put a Kleenex over it with a rubber band or something so it won't foam out all over the place. Watch it, and when it's foaming real good, which takes maybe eighteen to twenty-four hours, then you dump that in because the yeast has already started. Then you stir that in, and I've never had a stuck fermentation. I've never had a fermentation that just didn't take off like gangbusters.

I pretty much store my wine in 5-gallon jugs and then, as they get down to where there's not much of it left, I put it in gallon jugs and put labels on it and store it like that. I do bottle it up in normal-sized bottles, maybe three dozen wine bottles with my name and label, and give it to friends and so forth.

[*Mr. Dobbins points at some wine in storage.*] Actually that wine is not fermenting anymore. That's really just being stored and, as you see, the jugs are not full. We just siphon [the top] off whenever we want some wine of that particular kind. [I have two jugs sitting side by side.] One jug is right and the other one I can play with a little. I can gradually put some of the ["right" wine] into the other jug and [vice versa]. That way I have control of the sweetness. If I get one too sweet, I can juggle back and forth. [I put paper bags over the jugs] to preserve the color. You have sunlight coming through those windows from about three o'clock on. And the sunlight will cause wines to fade. I haven't noticed it, but experts claim it will affect the taste.

The hardest thing about making wine is that it takes time.

"So now I have almost a pint of pokeberry wine down in my cellar waiting for the return (if ever) of my sciatica."

~A. J. MAYER~

Midway through the preparation of this book, Margie Bennett discovered this letter in the Foxfire files. It is used with the permission and encouragement of Mr. Mayer's son, A. J. Mayer, Jr., also of Rockville, Virginia. The letter is dated March 1974.

Mr. Arthur Gordon
c/o Baltimore Sunday Sun

In the literary digest for November 1973, "The Magic Glow of Foxfire" gave me a little shove, to bother somebody about something that I learned from an old codger (a black old codger) in 1921. I am now 83 y/ol years old (that is natural shorthand for y/ears ol/d, it is learned only when you get old enough to write slower than you think, or you might say "think faster than you write even though you can no longer think fast"). In 1921 I lived in that part of Surry County, Virginia, whose most elite crop (I'm a farmer) next to Smithfield Ham was Virginia Runner Peas, the peanut, which after roasting were put in little 10¢ paper bags and sent all over the world to make little boys happy.

In 1921, about March as I remember it, I was almost incapacitated (in this case, "ham-strung" might be a more apropos word) by an attack of sciatica. The medicine I got at our local drugstore didn't seem equal to the task of getting rid of the sciatica. One day an old friend (I had known him about a year, but I call him old because he *was old*, and if there had been Social Security, he would have been collecting it, and incidentally he was a Baltimore man named Devries, a real Southern gentleman of the Old School. I'm a damn Yankee myself, God bless 'em.) Well anyhow, this nice old friend noticed my affliction (I was using two canes to get around) and strictly on his own, out of the goodness of his heart (are all Baltimore people that kind and compassionate?), he went to an old colored man he had known lots longer than he had known me—he had to drive twelve miles and back to do it, in his trusty Model T—and brought me 2 quarts of homemade pokeberry wine that he said was good for sciatica. (He was wrong there, because it was very bad for it: In just a couple of days the misery was entirely gone.) I had used up only about 20 spoonfuls of it, and I never had a recurrence of the sciatica. But the memory of the pokeberry wine, which was highly, enjoyably potable, has lingered with me until the spring of 1972 when I had a few twinges that reminded me of that old devil sciatica, so when in 1973 up here in Hanover County, Virginia, (God bless her) I had another visit(ation would be a better word) from sciatica I knew just where to get some pokeberries, about a quart-and-a-half, and made me some pokeberry wine. But I never even tasted the wine, because I couldn't wait for it to become wine, I just used it as soon as it had been processed, and stains were still on my fingers, and I used only 7 or 8 spoonfuls and lo! and behold! the sciatica was gone.

So now I have almost a pint of pokeberry wine down in my cellar waiting for the return (if ever) of my sciatica. I must admit that the wine tasted better than the pokeberry juice did (sugar added). I'm waiting for the next pokeberry harvest before I drink the p-b wine I have, because *if* the sciatica should return I wouldn't know where to get any more. In the years since I first knew about pokeberry wine I have given it to three or four other people who were suffering from sciatica. In fact I mailed some

(4 quarts) to my brother in Milwaukee when he had a dose of sciatica, and it worked just as good in Wisconsin as it had in Virginia. My brother lived to be 92 years old, but I don't know whether the pokeberry wine should be given the credit for that or not. But he was 10 years older than my father when *he* died, so it must have helped a little. My brother slipped on an icy street on New Year's Eve while walking to visit a friend to see the New Year in, and he broke a hip and died of pneumonia.

In making pokeberry wine, you macerate the berries in a little water and strain out all the pulp. The seeds and the roots of pokeberry are dangerously poisonous.

The other item for Foxfire friends is Woods Dittany as a cure for poison ivy. The whole plant (of the Dittany) is used, either fresh or dried (it will keep potent for years after being dried), as an embrocation, externally, and usually two or three applications is sufficient.* I once knew of some "city" boys who laid down in some poison ivy and after they got over the blisters and the itching they took the first train back to Syracuse N.Y. where they said poison ivy doesn't grow. (Like the snakes in Ireland? My grandmother came from Ireland, and *she* used to say the only snakes there came out of a bottle.)

There was a third item I had for Foxfire, but it has slipped my mind. So many things have slipped my mind these days, things that in my earlier days never slipped my mind. Like down in Surry County years ago, when there was no more shoulder (smoked hog shoulder) meat in the smokehouse, the farmers just

---

* *Woods Dittany (also referred to as Mountain Dittany, stone mint, wild basil, and Maryland Cunila) is a perennial herb native to the eastern United States, North Florida to New York, and as far west as Texas and Missouri. It grows in dry, stony woodlands, thickets, and open hillsides. Pleasantly mint-like, it is an attractive, small bushy plant with rose-purple, pinkish-to-white flowers literally covering the plant and attracting bees. After being dried and steeped for tea, it was used by both the American Indians and early settlers from Europe for common colds, headaches, fevers, colic, nervous infections, and as a beverage. When warmed, the tea is diaphoretic—it causes perspiration.*

We were unable to confirm its effectiveness against poison ivy.

took an axe and chopped some chips out of the rafters of the smokehouse and threw them in with the "greens" to flavor them while they were cooking. That's not true. They used shoulder meat for greens alright, but they always had kept some hams back for when their city kinfolks came to visit. The farmers I knew preferred jowls or shoulders, they thought they had better flavor. I do, too, but, when you are being nice to city folks you always feed 'em on ham. (And they never heard of chitlins either.)

All my apologies. I'm a long winded old coot.

A. J. Mayer
Rockville, Virginia

FOR BEST RESULTS

INTRODUCTION

The winemakers interviewed for this book have developed techniques that assure success. They only hint at failures. It was very instructive, therefore, for us to witness one unsuccessful attempt. Effie Lord, owner for several decades of a serve-yourself-in-the-kitchen cafe in downtown Clayton—and a lively source for many interviews on many subjects—tried to make pumpkin wine.

> I heard about this from some ol' man in south Georgia— was somebody talking about what he eats, you know, and talking about drinking pumpkin wine. So that's where I got the idea. But he didn't say how he made it. Talking about how it made a "muss." He just had a fit to make it, you know? Just made a lot of fuss—about living out in the wilderness and all. He wouldn't know nothin' about putting yeast in it, would he?
>
> I told the boys to come over here and cut that pumpkin out there [*points to storage room*]—little one, you know. Can't find nobody that knows how to cut it so I can put the stuffin' back in the pumpkin. I need somebody to cut it so I can put the "lid" back on it. [*Looks at Joseph, who is conducting the interview.*] You'll need a sharp knife, won't you? [*Joseph cuts the top off as if it were to be a jack-o'-lantern. Effie scrapes seeds and pulp from the*

Effie Lord

inside of the pumpkin.]

    I'm going to make it inside. I'm gonna put one cup of sugar in here and then put the top back on it. I don't know how sweet a pumpkin is. I think those small ones are supposed to be sweet. Let's put some little more sugar in there. [*Adds another cup.*] I'll just set it somewhere around—wherever I find a place to put it, and see how it does. [*Sets it in a corner of the storage room.*]

On a follow-up visit to check on Effie's rhubarb wine (a success) and the pumpkin experiment, Effie told us that the pumpkin had spoiled—smelled so bad she had thrown it out.

Many wine recipes probably began with experiments like Effie's, and there were probably many disasters. Mistakes do happen and wine does not always turn out as expected. What follows are some tips for improving the chances of making good wine.

EQUIPMENT

Containers

Never use metal containers, bowls, or spoons—the acids in the wine will react with the metals and produce chemicals that may be harmful. Wood and glass are preferred. Plastic is acceptable, though it may impart a slight plastic flavor to the wine. Avoid colored plastics.

> CARLTON ENGLISH: You need a churn—it's the best. Just an old clay churn seems to do. You can take a gallon of berries and you can use a gallon glass, say, a pickle jar or a milk jar, and that will work real good for 1 gallon of wine.

Equipment Sterilization

Churns, jars, and other equipment must be sterilized or must be at least *very* clean. This helps prevent "bad" bacteria from ruining your wine. The most common bacterial infection in wine is from *Acetobacter,* which turns wine into vinegar (acetic acid).

There are several easy methods of sterilization:

1. Pour boiling water over all surfaces of your equipment. The water

Common containers—a plastic trash can and a demijohn with an air lock

must be boiling to be effective. Do not pour the water over cool glass—it might shatter.

2. Household bleach can be diluted at 1 cup per gallon of water and used to sterilize the equipment. Do not use on metal equipment—it will corrode it. *Be sure everything is well rinsed with water that has been boiled and cooled—any traces of bleach will ruin wine.*

3. Eight Campden™ tablets can be crushed and added to 1 pint of cold water. (The Campden™ tablets will not be effective with hot water.) Use the same way as bleach. Do not use on metal equipment and do not breathe the fumes. Equipment does not have to be immersed or filled with the solution, just shake and roll the solution all around the insides of the equipment. All sterilized equipment should be well rinsed with water that has been boiled and cooled.

Straining

Straining is important: The clearer the wine, the better the flavor. Each recipe contains the method of straining, but most use a cloth of some sort.

> NELSON CABE: I strain mine with white cloth. Some people take [womens'] stocking hoses—strain with that. Most people, when they make wine, they keep straining it off until it foams a little bit.

> ALBERT GREENWOOD: Now, you'll have to wash that cloth. Once in a while, it causes that pulp in those grapes to stick to it. The juice won't go through much. Just wash it out good. [Rinse with water.] It won't have enough water on it to hurt anything.

Hydrometer

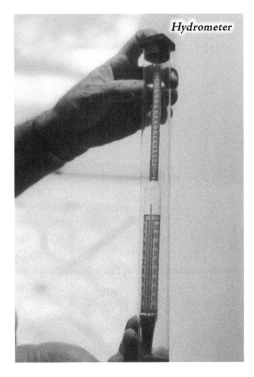

Hydrometer

The hydrometer is a device that measures the specific gravity of the wine. It is used by most experts and advanced wine makers, but it is not necessary for making wine. Specific gravity is a density measure and can be used to determine the amount of sugar in wine, hence the amount of alcohol in the final product. There are several types of hydrometers. The most useful for winemaking are those that have a Brix scale, enabling the user to measure both sugar and alcohol content. Hydrometers are available from winemaking supply houses.

Air Locks

One of the most useful devices for winemaking is the air lock. Its main purpose is to keep air out of the fermenting wine and yeast while, at the same time, permitting the escape of carbon dioxide.

> BILL PARK: That don't form a vacuum. It locks out the outside air, which contains wild yeast. Basically, you're locking out the wild yeast. If you let it ferment without an air lock on it, put a piece of cheesecloth over it to keep the bugs out. When you're making wine, if you don't have an air lock on tight, you have a lot of wineflies accumulate. You see some people have so many wineflies [that] they can't find the wine!

Several types of air locks are available in either glass or plastic and can be obtained through winemaking supply houses. Homemade air locks can be rigged, too, though they are cumbersome and unreliable.

> BILL PARK: With the old-fashioned way—this is why it's been improved—you never knew whether your wine was going to vinegar or not when you didn't cover it or do something with it. That's when they started making the little tube going from the glass jar to the bottle of water.

Air Lock

INGREDIENTS

Fruit

LUCY KIMBELL: Fall is a good time to make wine. Of course, you do it when the fruit is ready—it doesn't really matter the time of year. For this area, the grapes are better in the fall. In mid- or early-summer, you get plums and other fruits: peaches, blackberries, and things. From there on out, whenever fruit becomes available. You could make wine up to November.

Choose ripe fruit of good quality. Quality fruit makes quality wine. Rinse the fruit well before using. Cut out bruised areas and brown spots.

BILL PARK: The rule of thumb is: It takes a gallon of grapes to produce a gallon of wine. Some grapes have more natural sugar than others, and that's why French-type makes good wine. It's no good for eating. The different grapes make a different flavor. Some make it darker. And the riper the grapes, the darker the color and the riper the grapes, the better the wine.

Crushing or mashing the fruit exposes more surface area, improving both fermentation and flavor.

Bill Park and his grape press

The fruit should be sterilized to rid it of wild yeast bacteria. This can be done by pouring boiling water over the crushed fruit and sugar. Let the fruit-sugar-water mixture (sometimes called "must") cool before adding yeast or other ingredients. Use the amount of water called for in the recipe.

Sugar draws out the flavor of fruit. Though fruit-and-water mixtures will ferment on their own, sugar ensures better fermentation and flavor.

Water

If additional water is called for after the first fermentation, use boiled, cooled tap water. Do not use distilled water because distilling removes trace elements needed for yeast growth.

Sugar

Each pound of sugar in 1 gallon of must will produce about 5 percent alcohol by volume. The following shows the dryness of wine in proportion to the amount of sugar for each gallon of must:

About 1¾ pounds	Dry
About 2¼ pounds	Medium
Over 2¼ pounds	Sweet

Use the amount of sugar needed to obtain the desired level of alcohol, then sweeten to taste. More sugar should not be added until the wine is clear and all traces of yeast have been removed—otherwise, fermentation will begin again.

Yeast

General-purpose wine yeasts are preferable: They ferment rapidly and vigorously, they have a high tolerance for high levels of alcohol, they rapidly form a sediment when fermentation is complete, and they do not impart flavors to the wine. Bakers yeast (e.g., Fleischmann's™) can be used, but may leave a yeast flavor in the wine and may leave the wine slightly cloudy.

Starting the yeast before adding it to the must decreases the chance of infection in the wine. To start the yeast, boil ¼ pint water, ¼ cup sugar, and ¼ pint orange juice. Put in a sterilized glass jar with a screw-top lid. When the mixture has cooled to 68° to 77° F, add the yeast, cover and leave for about twelve hours at room temperature. Stir the yeast mixture into the must.

> CARLTON ENGLISH: You could put corn in it [instead of yeast] if you had sprouty corn. What they call malt. You sprout your corn and crush it up, and put it in there. That acts the same as yeast. Use about a teacupful of corn per gallon of wine. It won't change the taste much, just make it work a little better.

If you want to follow Carlton English's example, first you have to sprout corn as you would any sprouted seed: cover with water until sprouts appear and the seed becomes tender. Be sure to change the water at least once a day to prevent fermentation. Crush the sprouted corn with a food mill or grinder.

Loaded grape press hopper

PROCEDURES

Fermentation ("Working Off")

There are different views on what season is best for fermenting wine. Lawton Brooks advises: "It's better to make wine in the summertime. Warm as it is nowadays, like it's been a'being—good God, you put it up today and tomorrow, that stuff will start working. You just want to set it in the shade where it will be cool." Lucy Kimbell prefers the fall, when the days drop to the "ideal temperature"—about 70° F.

When fermenting wine, there are several things to remember:

1. When you pour the must into the churn or jar, always leave 2 or 3 inches from the top to allow room for bubbling.

2. Do not cap the container tightly. The pressure of the gases during fermentation might burst the container. (This is another reason for using an air lock.)

3. You may cover the must with a cloth to keep the gnats out of the wine, but be sure to fasten the cloth securely onto the churn. As Lucy Kimbell says, "You always keep that covered to keep the varmints out—the gnats and things like that it draws."

4. To prevent cloudiness in the finished wine, add commercially-prepared pectin-destroying enzyme to the cool must at the beginning of

fermentation. Pectic enzyme is available under several trade names at retail winemaking stores.

Racking, or Clearing the Wine

After the wine has finished fermenting and the pulp is out, let the wine sit so any suspended matter settles on the bottom. Place a clean, sterile jar of the same size approximately 1½ feet below and siphon with a small tube from the upper jar to the lower one. Do not disturb the sediment—keep the end of the tube in the upper jar above the sediment on the bottom.

Dissolve one Campden™ tablet in each gallon of wine. This ensures that the wine will keep well. Let sit until any suspended matter left is settled on the bottom. Siphon again. Then strain through a sieve with almost microscopically small holes. This removes suspended matter and leaves a clear wine. Then sweeten to taste.

Bottle Corker

Storage

Most wines do become better with age. It is recommended to store wine in a churn or demijohn for a while before bottling it. After bottling, store for six months or more in a cool, but not cold, place before opening. Do not store wine in plastic—it absorbs the plastic taste. Glass wine bottles with cork stoppers are the best containers. (Be sure to sterilize them.) Dissolve Campden™ tablets in the wine before bottling—one tablet to each gallon of wine.

Efficient storage

A NOTE ON LEGALITY

Federal law allows the home production of wine for home consumption—not for sale—of up to 200 gallons per family (two or more legal-aged adults) per year, or up to 100 gallons for a single legal-aged adult. Stay within those limits and you pay no taxes on the wine.

The relevant statute is 27CFR24.75—Code of Federal Regulations, Title 27, Part 24, Subpart C, Section 24.75 (*http://edocket.access.gpo.gov/cfr_2003/aprqtr/27cfr24.75.htm*). Direct inquiries to the Bureau of Alcohol, Tobacco, Firearms, and Explosives, Office of Public and Governmental Affairs, 99 New York Ave. NE, Mail Stop 5S144, Washington, DC 20226.

Important: Some states and localities have their own laws regarding winemaking, including the legal age at which an individual is considered an adult. Consult your local authorities for information specific to your area.

RECIPES

WINES

Minnie Taylor's Recipe for Blackberry Wine

EQUIPMENT
5-gallon churn
cloth
thin curtains or cheesecloth
half-gallon jars

INGREDIENTS
2 gallons berries
enough sugar so berries aren't too sweet and aren't too tart
1 pack yeast
water

PROCEDURE
Put berries, sugar, and yeast in churn. Add about 1 or 2 gallons of warm water, leaving 2 or 3 inches at the top. Tie cloth over the churn to keep out the bugs and let ferment until bubbling stops. Strain with thin curtains or cheesecloth. Pour wine into jars and set in a cool place for about two weeks.

Frances Lipe's Recipe for Blackberry Wine

EQUIPMENT
> *crock*
> *boiler*
> *thin cloth*
> *siphon*
> *demijohn*

INGREDIENTS
> *7 quarts berries*
> *1 egg white*
> *5½ quarts water*
> *7 pounds sugar*

PROCEDURE

Mash berries and add 3½ quarts water. Let stand for twenty-four hours, then strain through thin cloth.

Beat egg white in boiler, add sugar and 2 quarts water. Boil five minutes and skim. Cool, then add to the juice, stirring well.

Cover with the cloth. Skim and stir each morning for ten days. Leave until fermentation ceases, then siphon off and bottle in the demijohn.

Scott Brooks' Recipe for
Blackberry and Elderberry Wine

EQUIPMENT
> *5-gallon jug*
> *strainer*
> *balloon*
> *corks and bottles*

INGREDIENTS
> *1 gallon elderberries (include some greener berries that aren't quite ripe)*
> *1 gallon blackberries (include some berries which aren't quite ripe)*
> *4 pounds sugar*
> *1 quart honey*
> *water*
> *9 Campden™ tablets*
> *1 package unflavored gelatin*

PROCEDURE

Mash and strain berries. Measure juice and pour into jug. Add sugar, honey, and 1 quart warm water. Add Campden™ tablets and enough water to make the entire volume about 4½ gallons. Put balloon over the mouth of the jug and let it ferment for two weeks.

This wine will be slightly bubbly. To reduce the bubbles, put gelatin in it: Let the gelatin dissolve in water (amounts according to the gelatin package) for an hour, then boil it for fifteen or twenty minutes. Cool to room temperature and pour into the wine.

To bottle the wine, put olive oil on the bottoms of the corks and slide the corks into the bottles. Store at 65° to 75° F.

*Scott Brooks mashing blackberries through a strainer (above),
and showing the bottom of the strainer afterwards (below).*

*Scott Brooks pouring fresh juice (above), and adding honey
(instead of yeast) to aid fermentation (below).*

Mary Pitts' Recipe for Blackberry, Grape, or Whatever Wine

EQUIPMENT
> *2-gallon jar*
> *cheesecloth*
> *cotton cloth*
> *jars or bottles*

INGREDIENTS
> *about 2 gallons fruit*
> *water*
> *5 pounds sugar*

PROCEDURE

Put fruit in jar and add about 2 quarts water and 4 cups sugar, leaving 3 or 4 inches at the top. Let it ferment for two or three weeks, until the mixture finishes bubbling. Crush fruit and pour through cheesecloth. Measure juice: You should get 2 gallons of juice out of 2 gallons of berries and the water and sugar. Pour back into jar, and add 2 more cups sugar. Tie cotton cloth around the mouth of the jug and let ferment for about a week.

Pour juice through cheesecloth, pour back into jar, and add another cup of sugar. Let it ferment for about another week. Do this two more times, about a week apart, adding a cup of sugar each time and stirring well to dissolve the sugar. Strain wine and pour into quart jars. Tighten lids, then give one turn back—if fermentation isn't complete, jars won't burst. It will take three months to age.

Allison Adams (left) helps Mary Pitts strain blackberries through cheesecloth (above), and observes as Mary ties cheesecloth over the churn's mouth to keep out insects (below).

Arlyn Park's Recipe for Concord, Muscadine, and Fox Grape Wine

EQUIPMENT

5-gallon plastic bucket
grape press or sieve
5-gallon glass jug with air lock
jars or bottles

INGREDIENTS

approximately 1 bushel grapes
1 yeast cake
5 pounds sugar
water

PROCEDURE

Pick out the bad and the green grapes. Wash and mash the grapes. Put in bucket and add yeast. Let ferment for three days. Separate the pulp from the juice with the grape press or sieve. Be sure you get a full 1½ gallons of juice. Pour the juice in the 5-gallon glass jug. Over the next ten days, add 1 pound of sugar every other day, placing the sugar in just enough water to dissolve it, until 5 pounds have been added. After the ten days—once all the sugar has been added—add water to the jug, a quart at a time, until the jug is almost full. Bottle and store.

Clarence Lusk's Recipe for Corncob Wine

EQUIPMENT
> *3-gallon churn*
> *cloth strainer*
> *jars or bottles*

INGREDIENTS
> *enough fresh corn to yield 2½ to 3 gallons of sheared yellow corncobs*
> *water*
> *3 pounds sugar*
> *1 yeast pack*

PROCEDURE

Shear corn off cob. Pack cobs in the churn and add enough water to cover the cobs, leaving 3 or 4 inches at the top. Let it ferment for eight or nine days. Take cobs out and strain. Wash churn, put the juice back in, and add 1½ pounds sugar. Dissolve the yeast in a cup and pour into churn. Let it ferment for ten days. To make the wine more alcoholic, add another 1½ pounds sugar and let it ferment for another nine or ten days. Bottle the wine, but not too tightly.

Brown paper sacks protect working wine from sunlight

Granny Toothman's Recipe for Dandelion Wine

EQUIPMENT
    5-gallon stone crock
    strainer
    light, porous cloth
    jars or bottles

INGREDIENTS
    1 gallon yellow dandelion blossoms, without stems
    2 gallons boiling water
    5 to 6 pounds sugar
    sliced lemon
    2 sliced oranges, peeling and all

PROCEDURE
Put blossoms in crock and pour boiling water over them. Add 3 pounds sugar, sliced lemon, and sliced oranges. Cover with porous cloth and let ferment for three days. Strain mixture and add 2 or 3 pounds sugar. Cover with porous cloth and let ferment for at least nine days in a warm place. Strain and bottle. Don't cork too tightly or the bottle will burst.

Granny Toothman's Recipe for Elderberry Wine

EQUIPMENT
5-gallon stone jar
thin cloth
cheesecloth
jars

INGREDIENTS
1 gallon elderberries
3 pounds sugar

PROCEDURE

Strip the berries off the branches, wash them, and mash until soft. Add 1 pound sugar. Pour into jar and cover with cloth. Let ferment for three days. Strain through cheesecloth. Add the rest of the sugar and let it ferment. When it stops bubbling, store in jars and let sit for six months.

Teresa Thurmond

Frances Lipe's Recipe for Elderberry Flower Wine

EQUIPMENT
> 5-gallon crock or jar
> cheesecloth
> keg
> bottles

INGREDIENTS
> 1 quart elderberry flowers
> 9 pounds sugar
> 3 gallons water
> 2 cakes yeast
> 2 teaspoons lemon juice
> 3 pounds raisins

PROCEDURE

Cut flowers from stems with scissors and put flowers into crock. Boil sugar in water until dissolved, then pour over flowers. Cool. Add yeast and lemon juice.

After nine days, strain through double cheesecloth into keg. Add raisins, cover, and shake vigorously. Shake daily for about four or five days. Set on a firm surface, out of the way. Do not disturb for about six months, then bottle and store.

R. C. Dobbins' Recipe for Fox Grape and Muscadine Wine

EQUIPMENT
> *5-gallon plastic container with air lock*
> *5-gallon plastic container with a breather cap*
> *hydrometer*
> *siphon*
> *jars or bottles*

INGREDIENTS
> *about 4½ gallons berries*
> *water*
> *sugar*
> *5 Campden™ tablets (1 per gallon of juice)*
> *1 pint orange juice*
> *1 yeast cake*
> *Speedy Bentinite™*

PROCEDURE

Mash berries and put in container. Cover the berries with water. Add sugar until you get a specific gravity reading of 1.01 on hydrometer. Measure juice and add the Campden™ tablets. Cover and let sit for forty-eight hours.

Dilute orange juice with water, in a separate container, so that you have a quart of juice. Add 1 cup sugar and the yeast, according to instructions on the package. Cover with a tissue or cloth so the mixture won't foam over, and let sit for eighteen to twenty-four hours. Add to grape mixture, then put on the air lock and let ferment for eight to ten days. Siphon into the other 5-gallon container and put the breather cap on. Let ferment until bubbling stops. Add the Speedy Bentinite™, following directions on the package. Bottle the wine. Store in a cool place.

Minyard Conner's Recipe for Fruit Wine

EQUIPMENT
> *10-gallon wooden barrel*
> *strainer*
> *jars or bottles*

INGREDIENTS
> *enough fruit so there will be 2 or 3 inches from*
> *   the top when the fruit is covered with water*
> *up to 5 pounds sugar*
> *1 yeast cake*

PROCEDURE

Mash fruit, put into barrel, and let it ferment. When it finishes bubbling, strain the juice. Sweeten the juice and let it ferment again: for an 8- or 10-gallon jug add 1 pound sugar; for strong wine add ½ pound sugar to the gallon. Add yeast. Put the barrel in a cool place to ferment. In warm weather, the wine will ferment quicker and if it's cool it will take longer. If it's hot it should take a week or two to ferment. Bottle and store.

The finished product

Lucy Kimbell's Recipe for Fruit Wine

EQUIPMENT
> *8-gallon vat*
> *slotted wooden spoon*
> *thick towel*
> *hydrometer*
> *colander*
> *cheesecloth*
> *5-gallon glass jug with air lock*
> *siphon*
> *corker*
> *corks*
> *wine bottles*

INGREDIENTS
> *5 gallons crushed fruit*
> *4 Campden™ tablets*
> *5 pounds sugar*
> *1 package wine yeast*
> *Sparkolloid™ (optional)*
> *Sorbistat™*

PROCEDURE

Put fruit in vat. Mash fruit against the sides with the slotted spoon. Add 4 crushed Campden™ tablets, all of the sugar, and the yeast. Cover with towel and let ferment for five to seven days, stirring ingredients daily. Check the wine each day with the hydrometer while it is fermenting—keep the alcohol content at 22 percent. Strain through colander to get out the pulp, then strain the juice through the cheesecloth.

Pour the juice into the 5-gallon jar with the air lock. Let ferment until bubbling stops, then siphon. Mix the Sparkolloid™, if wanted, with the wine. Put the air lock back on and let the wine settle. Siphon and let settle as often as needed until wine is of desired clarity and appearance. Add Sorbistat™, which stops fermentation, and leave for one day. Bottle and cork wine.

Scott Brooks' Recipe for Grape Wine

EQUIPMENT
> *1-gallon jug*
> *balloon*
> *jars or bottles*

INGREDIENTS
> *2 12-ounce cans Welch's grape juice*
> *4 cups sugar*
> *¼ teaspoon yeast*

PROCEDURE

Pour grape juice into jug. Add sugar and yeast. Put balloon over the mouth of the jug, shake it up, and let it ferment for two weeks. Bottle and cork.

R.C. Dobbins discussing the clarity of wine

Nelson Cabe's Recipe for Grape Wine

EQUIPMENT
> *5-gallon wooden churn with lid*
> *cloth*
> *approximately 30-inch hose pipe*
> *paraffin wax*
> *old window netting or cheesecloth*
> *jars or bottles*

INGREDIENTS
> *crushed grapes to fill the churn to within 2 or 3 inches of the top*
> *up to 10 pounds sugar*
> *1 quart water*

PROCEDURE

Mash grapes with your hands and put in churn. Add 5 pounds of sugar. Cover with cloth, and put the lid on top. Slit a hole in the cloth and stick the hose through the hole. Pour the wax around and on top of the hose to seal off the hole. Place the other end of the hose in the quart of water. Let ferment until the water stops bubbling.

Take off the lid and strain the juice through the window netting or cheesecloth. Pour juice back in the jar and add less sugar than the first time, tasting to make sure the wine isn't too sweet (about 1 pound of sugar per gallon of juice). Let ferment for seven days.

Strain juice. Pour back into churn and add enough sugar so wine isn't too sweet and isn't too tart. Let ferment. Strain and add sugar so wine is of desired taste, then let ferment until water stops bubbling. Pour into jars and let sit for a few days, with tops screwed on lightly so the jars won't burst. Tighten tops, then store.

Carlton English's Recipe for Grape Wine

EQUIPMENT
10-gallon wooden barrel

INGREDIENTS
5 gallons grapes
5 pounds sugar plus 2 cups
1 gallon water plus additional water as needed
1 pack yeast or 1 teacup sprouted corn

PROCEDURE
Combine grapes, 5 pounds of sugar, 1 gallon of water, and yeast or sprouted corn in the barrel. Add water to fill barrel to within 3 inches of the top. Cover and store in a cool place. Allow to ferment for ten to twelve days, or until bubbling stops. Add 1 cup sugar, add water to fill the barrel to within 3 inches of the top, then ferment again until bubbling stops. Repeat the last step (third fermentation). Strain and bottle, leaving caps loose for six to twelve days, then tighten. Store in a cool place.

Fresh bottle corks

Bill Park's Recipe for Grape Wine

EQUIPMENT
> 5-gallon plastic bucket
> hydrometer
> cheesecloth
> siphon
> bottles

INGREDIENTS
> about 4½ gallons grapes
> sugar

PROCEDURE

Wash and crush grapes. Separate the pulp from the juice. Using the hydrometer, add sugar to the juice until you have a reading of 22. Cover with cheesecloth to keep out the bugs and let ferment until bubbling stops. Siphon wine into new bottles and let it age in the dark for at least six to eight months to a year.

Grover Webb's Recipe for Grape Wine

EQUIPMENT
5-gallon jar
strainer or colander
bottles

INGREDIENTS
approximately 3 gallons grapes
1½ gallons water
10 pounds sugar
1 yeast cake or 1 package yeast

PROCEDURE

Mash grapes and mix with water in the churn or jar. Add 5 pounds sugar and the yeast. Stir and cover. Ferment until bubbling stops, then strain out the pulp. Add the other 5 pounds sugar. Ferment until bubbling stops. Strain again and bottle. Store in a cool place.

Grover Webb and Donna Ramey

Albert & Ethel Greenwood's Recipe for Muscadine Wine

EQUIPMENT
> *potato masher*
> *5-gallon stone jar*
> *cloth*
> *cloth strainer*
> *aluminum foil*
> *jars*

INGREDIENTS
> *about 4½ gallons crushed grapes*
> *sugar*

PROCEDURE

Crush grapes with potato masher and put in stone jar. Fasten cloth around the jar to keep the bugs out. Let ferment in a warm place for three days. Pour juice through cloth strainer. Twist the cloth until all the juice is strained. Measure the juice: For 3 parts of juice, add 1 part of sugar. Stir until sugar is dissolved. Cover jar with aluminum foil and let sit for three or four weeks. Make sure bubbling has stopped, then pour into jars and screw tops on loosely. Tighten lids before storing.

Albert Greenwood and Chet Welch

Muscadine grapes on the vine

Lawton Brooks' Recipe for Muscadine or Blackberry Wine

EQUIPMENT
5-gallon churn
cloth for straining
cheesecloth
jars or bottles

INGREDIENTS
5 gallons fruit
about 10 pounds sugar

PROCEDURE
Mash fruit in small amounts in the churn. Cover and let it ferment for three days. Strain through cloth. Measure the juice and add 2½ to 3 pounds of sugar per gallon of juice. Tie cheesecloth around the top and let it ferment for three days. Bottle and cork the wine.

Christine Wigington's Recipe for Peach Wine

EQUIPMENT
½-gallon fruit jar
cloth for straining
jars or bottles

INGREDIENTS
sliced fresh peaches
water
sugar

PROCEDURE
Wash, peel, and slice peaches and put in the jar, filling jar to within 2 or 3 inches of the top. Cover with water. Add sugar until peaches are of desired taste—sweeten like you would to eat them. Put lid on but not too tightly. Let ferment until bubbling stops. Strain. Wine is ready to drink.

John Bulgin's Recipe for Rhubarb Wine

EQUIPMENT
>5-gallon jug
>5 plies of cheesecloth
>rubber band
>a piece of board
>cloth for straining
>rag or press
>gallon jugs
>corks

INGREDIENTS
>2 gallons chopped rhubarb
>2 gallons warm water
>4 pounds sugar
>1 package Fleischmann's Yeast™
>cornmeal

PROCEDURE

Mix the rhubarb, water, and sugar in the jug, leaving about 2 or 3 inches at the top. Add yeast and then cover the mixture with cornmeal. Cover the jug with the cheesecloth, fastening it to the neck of the jar with the rubber band, and then put the board on top. Let ferment for seven to nine days. Strain juice through cloth, then squeeze rhubarb in a rag or press to get extra juice. Add a little sugar so wine is a little tart, not too sweet. Put a fresh cheesecloth around the mouth of the jug and fasten with rubber band. Let wine ferment again. Stir the wine every day while it is fermenting. When it stops bubbling, leave the wine covered and let it sit to make sure it has finished fermenting. Pour wine into gallon jugs and cork. Store wine in a cool place.

Rhubarb must

Grover Webb's Recipe for Rhubarb Wine

EQUIPMENT
5-gallon jar
strainer or colander
jars or bottles

INGREDIENTS
4 gallons peeled and finely chopped rhubarb
2 gallons water
10 pounds sugar
1 yeast cake or 1 package yeast

PROCEDURE

Mix together rhubarb, water, 5 pounds sugar, and yeast. Cover and let it ferment for seven days. Strain out rhubarb, add the other 5 pounds sugar, cover, and let it ferment for another seven days. Bottle and refrigerate. Improves with age.

Frances Lipe's Recipe for Rice Wine

EQUIPMENT
>2-gallon stone crock
>wooden spoon
>colander
>cloth filter

INGREDIENTS
>one 1-ounce box seeded raisins
>1 orange slice
>1½ pounds raw rice
>1 yeast cake
>2½ pounds granulated sugar
>1 gallon tepid water

PROCEDURE

Mix all ingredients in the stone crock and cover. Let stand for about three to four weeks, depending on the temperature. Stir daily with a wooden spoon the first week, every other day the second week, none at all the rest of the time.

Strain, let sit another day, then filter. Cover and let age at least six months before drinking.

Clarence Lusk's Recipe for Scuppernong Grape Wine

Scuppernong grapes are a type of fox grape. Though the two terms commonly are used interchangeably, "scuppernong" refers specifically to fox grapes found along the Scuppernong River in North Carolina.

EQUIPMENT
> 3-gallon jar
> wine strainer

INGREDIENTS
> 2½ to 3 gallons mashed grapes
> water
> 3 to 6 pounds sugar
> 1 packet yeast

PROCEDURE

Mash grapes with hands and put in jar. Cover with water until grapes are just floating, leaving about 2 or 3 inches at the top. Cover and let it ferment for eight or nine days. Strain in small quantities, occasionally emptying the pulp. Measure juice: Add 3 pounds sugar per gallon and add yeast. Cover jar and let ferment for at least ten days. Bottle the wine, but not too tightly.

JUICES

Nora Garland's Recipe for Apple Cider

EQUIPMENT
5-gallon churn
cloth for straining
gallon jars
canning lids
big bath boiler

INGREDIENTS
about 4 gallons apples
hot water
2 or 3 pounds sugar

PROCEDURE
Wash, cut, and core apples. Put in churn, and fill to within 2 or 3 inches of the top. Cover apples with hot water and let sit for a few days. Add sugar, cover, and let ferment until bubbling stops. Strain the cider through the cloth. Pour cider into jars, screw tops on loosely, and put in a hot-water bath for five to seven minutes or until the cider starts to boil. Seal jars.

Irene Ramey's Recipe for Berry Juice

EQUIPMENT
large pot
cloth bag
colander
1-gallon jar

INGREDIENTS
1 gallon berries
water to cover
1 cup sugar for each cup juice

PROCEDURE
Wash berries and put in the pot. Barely cover berries with water. Cook until berries are soft. Pour into cloth bag and squeeze the juice out. Pour the juice through the colander to make sure the seeds are out. Measure juice, add sugar, and store in the gallon jar in the refrigerator.

Mary Pitts' Recipe for Blackberry Juice

EQUIPMENT
container large enough to hold 8 to 10 quarts of berries
strainer
canning jars and lids

INGREDIENTS
8 to 10 quarts blackberries
water to cover

PROCEDURE
Put berries in pot with enough water to cover them. Let them simmer on the stove until all the berries break up. Strain juice, put back on the stove and let it come to a boil. Pour juice into quart jars and seal.

Nelson Cabe's Recipe for Grape Juice

EQUIPMENT
½-gallon jar, with lid
colander (optional)

INGREDIENTS
2 cups grapes
1 cup sugar
hot water to cover

PROCEDURE

Put grapes and sugar in the jar and pour hot water over the mixture. Seal the jar and put in a hot-water bath. Bring to a boil and cook for twenty minutes. After the juice has cooled, shake the jar to finish breaking up the berries. Leave the jar sealed and set aside for about two or three months, until the juice is all one color. Juice can be strained when ready to drink.

Nora Garland's Recipe for Grape Juice

EQUIPMENT
4- or 5-gallon pot
cloth for straining
jars and lids
large bath boiler

INGREDIENTS
2 gallons grapes
water to cover
sugar to taste

PROCEDURE

Wash grapes and put in pot. Cover with water and cook until grapes are soft. Strain juice and pour into jars and put the lids on. Put the jars in a hot-water bath for seven minutes or until the juice starts boiling. Take the jars out, cool, and tighten lids. Add sugar so juice is of desired sweetness before serving.

Minnie Taylor's Recipe for Grape Juice

EQUIPMENT
½-gallon glass jar, with lid
colander (optional)

INGREDIENTS
2 cups grapes
boiling water to cover
1 cup sugar

PROCEDURE

Wash grapes and pour into jar. Pour boiling water over the grapes until covered, then add sugar. Cover and let ferment for about 1 week, until bubbling stops. Let sit in a cool place for one or two weeks. Juice can be strained when ready to drink.

Irene Ramey's Recipe for Peach or Apple Juice

EQUIPMENT
large pot
strainer
boiler
1-gallon jar

INGREDIENTS
1 gallon fruit
water to cover

PROCEDURE

Peel fruit. Wash, cut the cores out, cut up the fruit, and put in pot. Barely cover the fruit with water. Cook until tender. Let sit until cool, strain, and pour into jars. Store in refrigerator.

OTHER BEVERAGES

Ervin Taylor's Recipe for Homebrew

EQUIPMENT
  5-gallon churn
  bottles or jars

INGREDIENTS
  about 2½ gallons hot water
  up to 10 pounds sugar
  1 quart can Blue Ribbon malt
  2 packs yeast
  1 Irish potato, peeled and cut into small pieces, or 1 large box raisins

PROCEDURE
Fill churn half full with hot water. Add 5 pounds of sugar, and the malt and yeast. Cover and let ferment until bubbling stops. Add raisins or cut-up potato to the mixture. Let ferment until bubbling stops. To double the alcoholic content, add 5 pounds of sugar and let ferment for ten more days or whenever bubbling stops. Bottle and store.

Melvin Taylor's Recipe for Homebrew

EQUIPMENT
> *5-gallon churn*
> *bottles or jars*

INGREDIENTS
> *one 5-pound can Blue Ribbon malt syrup*
> *10 pounds sugar*
> *handful grapes or raisins (optional)*
> *3 or 4 Irish potatoes, peeled and cut into small pieces*

PROCEDURE
Combine the malt syrup, 5 pounds sugar, the grapes or raisins (if desired), and the potatoes in the churn and cover. Ferment. Then add 5 more pounds sugar and let ferment again. Strain, bottle, and chill.

Granny Toothman's Recipe for Mead

EQUIPMENT
> *boiler or pot*
> *5-gallon stone jar*
> *thin cloth strainer*
> *bottles or jars*

INGREDIENTS
> *4 or 5 pounds honey*
> *water*
> *1 cake wine yeast*

PROCEDURE
Mix honey with 1 gallon hot water until honey is dissolved. Pour mixture into jar. Dissolve yeast in a little bit of lukewarm water and add to mixture. Cover the jar with a thin cloth and put in a cool, dark place for six months. After it has finished fermenting, strain it and bottle.

Nora Garland's Recipe for Persimmon Beer

EQUIPMENT
5-gallon churn
cloth for straining
canning jars and lids
large bath boiler

INGREDIENTS
about 2½ gallons persimmons
hot water to cover
4 pounds sugar
handful of honey locusts, or 1 pint honey

PROCEDURE

Gather persimmons while frost is on them. Cut in half and pit the fruit. Pour persimmons into churn, filling the churn about half full. Add hot water to cover the persimmons. Let the mixture sit two or three days, until persimmons are soft. Add 2 pounds sugar. Then add the honey, or break up honey locusts and add. Let ferment until honey locusts come to the top, or until bubbling ceases. Strain. Add the remaining 2 pounds sugar, and let ferment until beer is of desired taste. Stir beer every few days. Strain again. Pour the beer into jars and screw the lids on loosely. Place the jars in a hot-water bath, take out when the beer starts boiling, and seal the jars.

Christine Wigington's Recipe for Persimmon Beer

EQUIPMENT
>   *5-gallon churn*
>   *cloth*
>   *plate*
>   *bottles or jars*

INGREDIENTS
>   *about 1¼ gallons persimmons*
>   *equal amount honey locusts*
>   *hot water to cover*

PROCEDURE

Cut persimmons in half and break the locusts in half. Layer the persimmons and locusts in the churn, filling about half full. Pour hot water over them, leaving 2 or 3 inches at the top. Place cloth over the churn. Turn the plate upside down and put over the cloth. Let sit until beer is of desired taste. Strain, bottle, and store.

INDEX

~How You Can Help~

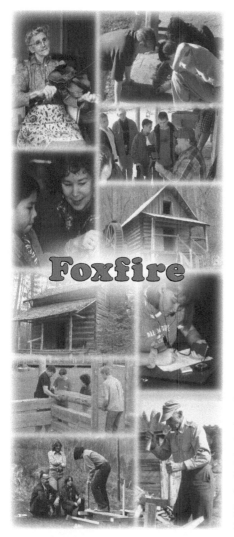

The Foxfire Fund, Inc., is a not-for-profit, educational and literary organization based in Rabun County, Georgia. Founded in 1966, Foxfire's learner-centered, community-based educational approach is advocated through both a regional demonstration site (the Museum and Heritage Center) grounded in the southern Appalachian culture that gave rise to Foxfire, and a national program of teacher training and support (the Foxfire Approach to Teaching and Learning) that promotes a sense of place and appreciation of local people, community, and culture as essential educational tools.

The books and magazines produced by our students are vital educational tools, for through the act of laboring to create quality end-products, our students not only learn basic academic and business skills, but also derive justifiable assurance of their competence, ability, and self-worth.

The sales and royalties from these products help support the wide range activities of our organization. The income from these products alone, however critical, covers only a portion of our annual budget. Income from our endowment, educational training and publications, and donations from individuals make up the balance of our expenses.

You can help Foxfire by purchasing our products, from either the Museum gift shop or our website, or by making donations to the Foxfire Museum, the magazine program, or our educational programs. Consider this: *The Foxfire Magazine* began in 1966 with one teacher, 140 students, and $440 in donations from community residents and businesses. The Foxfire Fund, Inc., has grown from that humble beginning into an internationally-known organization with over nine million books in print—your support of the students' work will go a very long way.

For more information, contact Foxfire by visiting www.foxfire.org, by email at foxfire@foxfire.org, by phone at 706-746-5828, by fax at 706-746-5829, or by mail at Post Office Box 541, Mountain City, Georgia 30562

~Other Foxfire Titles~

Aunt Arie: A Foxfire Portrait

This book *IS* Aunt Arie. In her own words, she discusses everything from planting, harvesting, and cooking to her thoughts about religion and feelings about living alone.

Appalachian Cookery

Over 500 unpretentious, delectable recipes combined with the wit and wisdom of those who have prepared and eaten such foods for generations, along with traditional preservation methods.

Appalachian Toys and Games

Part oral history and part rule book, a joyous collection of memories of playing indoor and outdoor games, each with complete instructions and the flavor of southern Appalachia.

A Foxfire Christmas

The memories shared here are from a simpler time, when gifts were fewer but perhaps more precious. Included are instructions for re-creating many of the ornaments, toys, and recipes that make up so many family traditions.

Wood Stove Cookery

Originally the Winter 1981 issue of *The Foxfire Magazine*, this book contains basic information for firing up and cooking on an old-fashioned wood stove, and contains over 100 recipes and methods for producing some of the best-tasting dishes you'll ever remember.